READ IT IN GREEK

Read It in Greek

An Introduction
to New Testament Greek

L. William Countryman

WILLIAM B. EERDMANS PUBLISHING COMPANY
GRAND RAPIDS, MICHIGAN / CAMBRIDGE, U.K.

First published 1993 as *The New Testament Is in Greek*
Reprinted with new title in 1998

02 01 00 99 98   6 5 4 3 2

Library of Congress Cataloging-in-Publication Data

Countryman, Louis William, 1941–
Read it in Greek: an introduction to New Testament Greek /
L. William Countryman.
p.   cm.
Includes index.
ISBN 0-8028-0665-1
1. Greek language, Biblical — Grammar.
2. Bible. N.T. — Language, style.   I. Title.
PA817.C68   1993
487′.4 — dc20   93-26629
CIP

*To my teachers and my students in Greek — often
the same people — this work is dedicated*

ΔΟΞΑ ΕΝ ΥΨΙΣΤΟΙΣ ΘΕΩ
ΚΑΙ ΕΠΙ ΓΗΣ ΕΙΡΗΝΗ
ΕΝ ΑΝΘΡΩΠΟΙΣ ΕΥΔΟΚΙΑ

CONTENTS

PREFACE

The present volume offers a one-semester introduction to the Hellenistic Greek language as used in the New Testament. It does not claim to work miracles — for example, to convey a year's worth of Greek in a single term or to offer the kind of facility with the language that can come only with years of reading. It has the limited goal of giving students with limited time for the language some ability to look behind the facade of modern-language translations, to deal at an elementary level with the Greek text, and to follow discussions in good commentaries and other scholarly works.

The method of the text is based on four basic principles:

1. The work centers on *reading* (the texts read are 1 John and, in the final lessons, 2-3 John and the prologue of John's Gospel) rather than on learning rules of grammar and syntax as if they were a kind of secret code by which language is to be deciphered.
2. The student learns more by *habituation* than by memorization, much as one learns one's own native language. Rote memorization is used only in limited ways to speed the process a little.
3. I have aimed at a "quick and dirty" transition from English to Greek grammar, rather than presenting a detailed and precise account of the latter according to any particular school of thought. *Problems of syntax are explained,* wherever possible, *in terms of English usage.*
4. I have integrated lessons in the *exegetical use of Greek* into the language course itself, rather than leaving exploration of exegesis entirely to future courses.

These principles emerged from my appraisal of the special circumstances for which I have created this text. They address a curricular
problem that seems to be widespread in American seminaries now: the
very limited amount of time available to most students for language
study, coupled with the virtual certainty that they will have had no
biblical language before coming to seminary. If a single semester of
Greek is to be of any value to the student, it needs to be a complete
entity in its own right, resulting in usable skills, not merely the first half
of a year-long course that most students will not, in fact, complete.

In addition to this curricular limitation, the teacher of Greek must
reckon with the fact that many American seminary students today are
adults returning to school after a substantial time away. Their experience
of engagement in productive work has created a strong desire to see
immediate purpose and relevance in what they are doing in the class-
room and perhaps a certain disinclination to plow through paradigms
on the promise that they will reap their reward many terms (or years)
in the future. These students are also often anxious that their memory
may be less agile and flexible than it once was. Whether or not this is
true, anxiety is itself a significant inhibiting factor in learning.

This text, then, is designed to introduce students to the *reading* of
New Testament Greek. It supports the reading process with some con-
centrated study in grammar and syntax, though without much memorization of paradigms. The method stresses the large picture and various
"rules of thumb" rather than encouraging a fastidious precision from
the beginning. Those students who go on to further Greek courses will
find it easy enough to refine the general concepts received here. Those
who do not can, in my experience, at least retain the basic ability to pick
up a Greek New Testament and make something of it.

There is a trade-off involved in teaching Greek by this method.
The advantage is that students can move quite quickly into actual reading and understanding of some relatively simple New Testament Greek.
The disadvantage is that they are thrown into the midst of a strange
medium of communication, rather like children learning their first
language, and this can prove very disorienting. Accordingly, the instructor who is teaching with the use of this text needs to be a cheerleader
and handholder more than the drill sergeant of some older methods.

Step-by-step methods, which never give the student anything to
read that has not first been fully explained, are, in some respects, easier.
They do not create quite the sense of vertigo that a method like the one

followed by this book can cause. On the other hand, more time passes before the student encounters an actual New Testament text, and such approaches require more memorization, are more daunting for many returning students, and, for most people, are less interesting to work through. On the whole, the rewards of the present approach outweigh any disadvantages.

To the Instructor

The most important thing for the instructor is to resolve from the beginning not to supplement this method with bits and pieces from more grammar-oriented methods. The two methods do not mix well, and it is easy to wind up overburdening students. For that matter, it is best not to "part the curtain" too much, offering explanations of things that have not yet arisen in the actual Greek texts being read. And on the whole, the grammatical explanations in the lessons follow a rational order — as well as being prompted by elements in the text of 1 John.

The lessons are not of equal length. Some, particularly those that introduce the Greek verb, will require more than one class session. They were created for a situation with the less-than-desirable regimen of two eighty-minute classes per week. Adjustments will have to be made where different schedules are followed, but the lessons are constructed so that it will be easy to disassemble them and put different segments on different days. It will probably be useful to follow Lesson X with a review.

Oral repetition is very important in learning a language. The eye alone cannot carry the burden. Students should be encouraged to practice aloud. The Greek text should always be read aloud in class — perhaps by the class as a whole to spare individuals who get anxious when asked to read on their own. It is also helpful to add other texts for memorization. (It is typically more productive to memorize texts rather than paradigms.) In addition to the liturgical texts in Lesson I, the Lord's Prayer is particularly useful for illustrating points of grammar and syntax. The instructor who is musically inclined may even wish to add some hymns. One possible source is Egon Wellesz, *The Music of the Byzantine Church* (Cologne: Arno Volk Verlag, 1959).

Any course that follows this book will be, especially from Lesson XI on, an introduction to exegesis of the New Testament as well as to the language of the New Testament. The reason for this is the thought that informed reading really is exegesis and that exegesis of the Greek text can be taught best in conjunction with the language itself.

Part of what this introduction to exegesis involves is introduction to some of the tools of exegesis. This is accomplished in the bibliography in Lesson XXII and, before that, in descriptions of the uses of some of the most basic tools in earlier lessons. It is assumed from Lesson V on that each student has easy access to the Bauer-Arndt-Gingrich-Danker *Greek-English Lexicon of the New Testament and Other Early Christian Literature* (the 1979 second edition). By Lesson VII each student should have a copy of the (corrected) third edition of the United Bible Societies' *Greek New Testament*. Use of Robert Van Voorst's *Building Your New Testament Greek Vocabulary* is first suggested in Lesson VII. And use of an analytical concordance such as *The Eerdmans Analytical Concordance to the Revised Standard Version of the Bible* is described beginning in Lesson XIX. Full bibliographical data on these works appears in the Lesson XXII bibliography.

Most single-semester courses will probably not get to the last two lessons. Those lessons can, however, be the first part of a second semester, which would then proceed to a quick review of grammar and syntax and to the reading of a New Testament work of moderate difficulty, such as Mark or John.

The instructor who is using this method will find that, beyond the basic business of organizing the class and keeping it in motion, her or his role will consist of reassurance, encouragement, reassurance, incidental explanations, reassurance, good humor, reassurance, repetition, and reassurance. It can be rather fun — and a good deal friendlier than the drill-sergeant business.

ACKNOWLEDGMENTS

This work owes much to contributions from students and faculty at Texas Christian University and, more recently, at The Church Divinity School of the Pacific and the Graduate Theological Union. It is my students in introductory Greek who, above all, have taught me how to teach it. I owe a particular debt to Prof. Rebecca Lyman, who had the daring and strength of nerve (foolhardiness?) to teach our shared Greek course one semester at CDSP while I produced the text, bringing her the lessons in batches. I am also indebted to CDSP for allowing Rebecca and me to coteach the course in that peculiar fashion. Earlier, at Brite Divinity School, I had the pleasure and profit of sharing Greek-teaching responsibilities with Prof. William Baird and learning from him. Prof. Daryl Schmidt read an earlier version of this work and, with his superior attainments in grammar, saved me from some errors and contributed useful observations. To Prof. Isaac Yerusalmi, my instructor in Aramaic and Syriac long ago at Hebrew Union College, Cincinnati, I owe the model for my title; my imitation is a gesture of profound respect for him and his teaching. Dr. Edgar W. Smith, Jr., and Dr. John W. Simpson, Jr., at Eerdmans have been most encouraging of this project. Whatever inadequacies this book still contains, despite so much help and encouragement, are, alas! still the responsibility of the author.

LESSON I

ΤΑ ΣΤΟΙΧΕΙΑ (Basic Elements)

The Greek language has a long history and naturally changed a good deal in the course of this history. The form of the language introduced in this primer was current in the Hellenistic and Roman periods, about 300 B.C.E. to about 600 C.E. It is sometimes called "Hellenistic" Greek, sometimes κοινή *(koinē)*, that is, "common." In the preceding era (the classical period) several quite distinct dialects of Greek were in use. The language of Hellenistic and Roman times was called "common" because it was basically the same everywhere that it was spoken. The New Testament documents were all written in this common language, though they vary in the degree of learning, complexity, and elegance that they exhibit.

The form of writing in use during the Hellenistic-Roman period consisted entirely of what we now call the "capital" letters. Most manuscripts had no punctuation or accent marks, and there were no divisions between words. Only later, in the Byzantine age, did such features become common — and with them the use of lowercase letters. But since all these features make reading Greek much easier, it is now normal for all literary texts, even ancient ones, to be printed in the later writing style. The elements of this writing style are presented in this chapter as the στοιχεῖα or "basic elements" for learning to read Greek.

Ο ΑΛΦΑΒΗΤΟΣ (The Alphabet)

We begin with the alphabet. The table below gives four kinds of information about each letter of the Greek alphabet:

1

- the capital and lowercase forms of the letter,
- its Greek name,
- the name transliterated (showing how one can substitute Roman letters for Greek ones when there is no convenient way to reproduce the Greek ones), and
- a guide to pronunciation.

Two types of pronunciation are offered here. The student should make a choice of one of the two and stick with it. Both are really reconstructions, since Greek is no longer spoken exactly as it was in antiquity. The reconstructed "classical" pronunciation is the one most commonly used in school settings; it tries to capture some of the basic sounds of Greek as it was spoken in about the fifth century B.C.E. The "Byzantine" pronunciation is closer to the pronunciation of Modern Greek and to the pronunciation of the liturgy of the Greek Church today. The pronunciation of the Hellenistic-Roman era was somewhere between the two.

Letter		Name	The name transliterated	Pronunciation "classical"	Byzantine
A	α	ἄλφα	alpha	cat, arch	
B	β	βῆτα	bēta	bet	vet
Γ	γ	γάμμα	gamma	go	aargh!
				anger*	
Δ	δ	δέλτα	delta	do	there
E	ε	ἒ ψιλόν	epsilon	extra	
Z	ζ	ζῆτα	zēta	adze	zoo
H	η	ἦτα	ēta	fame	tickle
Θ	θ	θῆτα	thēta	thistle	
I	ι	ἰῶτα	iōta	tickle	
K	κ	κάππα	kappa	kind	
Λ	λ	λάμβδα	lambda	love	
M	μ	μῦ	mu	maybe	
N	ν	νῦ	nu	nevertheless	
Ξ	ξ	ξῖ	xi	exit	
O	o	ὂ μικρόν	omikron	hop	

* Gamma has the sound of n when it is used before another palatal sound, i.e., γ, κ, ξ, and χ (g, k, x, and ch).

Π	π	πῑ	**pi**	party	
Ρ	ρ	ῥῶ	**rhō**	ride	
Σ	σ, ς*	σίγμα	**sigma**	sudden	
Τ	τ	ταῦ	**tau**	terrible	
Υ	υ	ὖ ψιλόν	**upsilon**	*rue* (French)	tickle
Φ	φ	φῖ	**phi**	fate	
Χ	χ	χῖ	**chi**	*achtung!*	
Ψ	ψ	ψῖ	**psi**	oo**ps**!	
Ω	ω	ὦ μέγα	**ōmega**	oh no!	drop

Diphthongs

The following vowel combinations (or "diphthongs") have pronunciations specific to them:

	classical	Byzantine
αι	**ai**sle	**e**dge
αυ	**ou**ch!	**av**alanche
ει	w**eigh**t	**ti**ckle
ευ	**Eu**rope†	**e**ver
ηυ	**heyyou**!	**gi**ve
οι	c**oi**n	**ti**ckle
ου	b**oo**t	b**oo**t
υι	**we**	**ti**ckle

The long vowels α (α can be short or long), η, and ω can also form diphthongs with ι, but the addition of ι did not change their pronunciation. Perhaps to indicate this, the iota is written *under* the other letter as an "iota subscript": ᾳ, ῃ, ῳ. Even though the iota subscript is not pronounced, it is important to note and remember it in reading and writing, for it often conveys important information about the meanings of words.

Breathings

The Greek alphabet has no letter for the "h" sound. The sound did exist, however, for a time. It appeared at the beginning of many words that start

---

* This form (ς), called "*final* sigma," is used only when sigma is the last letter of a word.
† But without the "y" sound at the beginning of "Europe."

with vowels and of all words that start with the letter ῥῶ. Such words are marked with a "rough breathing" (ʽ) placed over the initial vowel (before the vowel if it is a capital) or over the second vowel of an initial diphthong (in which case it is, nonetheless, pronounced before the diphthong). Not all words beginning with vowels had the "h" sound; those without it are marked with a "smooth breathing" (ʼ). The reconstructed classical pronunciation distinguishes between these. For example,

	ἀλλά	allá
	ἔχω	échō
	εὐχαριστία	eucharistía
	οἶκος	oíkos
but	ὅλος	hólos
	ὕδρα	húdra
	ἔξω	héxō
	υἱός	huiós

Note that in some instances breathing marks appear with accents (ʹ, ʼ, or ˜).

In Byzantine pronunciation, no distinction is made between the two breathing marks; the rough breathing is pronounced (or *not* pronounced!) just like the smooth. The rough breathing continues to be important, though, because it helps us distinguish between otherwise identical words and because it sometimes affects the spelling of the preceding word.

When transliterating a Greek word into Roman letters, use "h" to represent a rough breathing.

Accents

The classical Greek language had three pitch accents:

ʹ   *acute*, indicating a pitch about a fifth above the basic tone,
ˋ   *grave*, indicating a pitch perhaps a third above the basic tone,
˜   *circumflex*, indicating a pitch rising to a fifth (or starting there) and then falling to the basic tone.*

---

* Another form that the circumflex accent has in some texts (including the United Bible Societies' *Greek New Testament*) is ˆ.

In the Hellenistic-Roman period, these accents continued to be written
but were no longer differentiated in pronunciation. Few people attempt
to give them their singing quality today, and to do so would involve
some guesswork in any case. Instead, all three are treated in pronunciation like the stress accent used in modern English. Distinguishing among
the three forms is not a major element in this book, and here, at least,
accents are not represented in transliterations in any way. We will point
out a few items of particular importance from time to time, and a more
detailed account can be found in the fourth section of the paradigms
at the back of this book (pp. 198-200).

Punctuation and Other Signs

.   period, used as in English
·   colon, used like the English colon and semicolon
,   comma, used like the English comma
;   question mark (*not* semicolon)
᾽   apostrophe, indicating omission of one or more letters
¨   diaeresis, indicating that two successive vowels are to be read
    separately, not as a diphthong, e.g., Βηθσαϊδά, "Bethsaida"
    (Matthew 11:21), which has four syllables: *Bēth-sa-i-da.*

EXERCISES

1. Memorize the alphabet, both capital and lowercase letters, with their
names. Be able to write the letters out correctly in order. The chart below
may help you learn to write the lowercase letters correctly. Note that
alpha is more like a stylized "fish" than like the English "a."

ν ξ ο π ρ σ ς

π υ φ χ ψ ω

2. Practice reading the following aloud till they become easy for you:

Gloria patri:

> Δόξα τῷ πατρὶ καὶ τῷ υἱῷ καὶ τῷ ἁγίῳ πνεύματι,
> ὥσπερ ἐν ἀρχῇ καὶ νῦν καὶ ἀεὶ καὶ εἰς τοὺς αἰῶνας τῶν αἰώνων.
> ἀμήν.

Trisagion:

> Ἅγιος ὁ θεός,
> ἅγιος ἰσχυρός
> ἅγιος ἀθάνατος
> ἐλέησον ἡμᾶς

3. Transliterate the texts above into Roman letters; e.g., the Trisagion begins: Hagios ho theos. . . .

LESSON II

The best way to learn a language is to plunge in. You will learn best if you use ear and voice as well as eye. Learn to read the following verse aloud in Greek as fluently as you can; practice will eventually give you skill at this. Study the notes to see how much you can understand about the way the words fit together. (Words that occur more than once in a lesson appear only the first time in the notes.) Write down questions for your instructor. And do not expect to understand everything at once. Right now, you are at the stage of the one-year-old!

῝Ο ἦν ἀπ᾽ ἀρχῆς, ὃ ἀκηκόαμεν, ὃ ἑωράκαμεν τοῖς ὀφθαλμοῖς ἡμῶν, ὃ ἐθεασάμεθα καὶ αἱ χεῖρες ἡμῶν ἐψηλάφησαν, περὶ τοῦ λόγου τῆς ζωῆς —

Here is a transliteration that may help, particularly if you are using the reconstructed classical pronunciation:

Ho ēn ap᾽ archēs, ho akēkoamen, ho heōrakamen tois ophthalmois hēmōn, ho etheasametha kai hai cheires hēmōn epsēlaphēsan, peri tou logou tēs zōēs. . . .

---

* Lowercase α followed by the ′ mark (α′) is the numeral "one." This way of indicating numerals is explained further in the second paragraph of Lesson VII.

7

Each of the readings will be accompanied by notes to help you with particular words and phrases:

ὅ   a neuter form of the relative pronoun: *that which, what.*

ἦν   *was*

ἀπ' ἀρχῆς   *from beginning:* ἀπ', short for ἀπό, *from;* ἀρχῆς, from ἀρχή, *beginning*   We would say, "From *the* beginning," but Greek does not always use a definite article where English would like one.

ἀκηκόαμεν   *we have heard*   The subject "we" is indicated by the ending -μεν.

ἑωράκαμεν   *we have seen*

τοῖς ὀφθαλμοῖς   *with (by means of) the eyes*

ἡμῶν   *of us, our*   Greek often puts modifiers *after* the noun; English usually wants them *before:* with *our* eyes.

ἐθεασάμεθα   *we have observed*   The verb ending -μεθα, like -μεν, indicates that the subject is "we."

καὶ   *and*

αἱ χεῖρες   *the hands*

ἐψηλάφησαν   *[they] have handled*   The ending -αν indicates that the subject of the verb is third person plural. Here the subject is expressed by a noun ("hands") and therefore no pronoun is needed in the English translation.

περὶ τοῦ λόγου   *concerning the word*

τῆς ζωῆς   *of life,* literally "of the life"   Here Greek uses an article where English would not.

β' ΓΡΑΜΜΑΤΙΚΑ (Grammar)

"Person" and "Number" of Verbs*

An English verb can have three different sorts of "person" as subject: first person (speaker), second person (addressee), or third person (subject of conversation). Each of these "persons" can be singular (sg.) or plural (pl.) — a quality referred to as "number." Thus:

	sg.	pl.
1st person	I have	we have
2nd person	you have (thou hast)	you have
3rd person	he / she / it has	they have

Except in 3rd sg. (and the archaic 2nd sg.), English does not change the form of the verb to indicate person or number. Where there is no noun serving as the subject, we use pronouns (I, you, etc.) to indicate person and number. Greek, on the other hand, indicates person and number by means of endings attached to the verb. In this Lesson's reading we encountered two endings that indicate "we" (1st pl.): -μεν and -μεθα. We also encountered one 3rd pl. ending, -αν. We will be meeting other such "personal endings."

**Basic Sentence Types and What Goes into Them —
A Quick and Dirty Review**

In Greek, as in English, there are two basic types of sentences, and each has its own distinctive structure. The type of verb used determines which type of sentence we are dealing with. Verbs come in two basic varieties: linking verbs and action verbs. Linking verbs tell who or what the subject *is;* action verbs tell what the subject *does.*

    Linking verbs are few in number; but those few verbs tend to be very common and are used over and over again. In English the most common linking verbs are "be" and "become":

---

* If terms like "verb" and "noun" are giving you trouble, you will find help in the Glossary at the end of this book.

- Sarah *is* President.
- Sarah *becomes* President.
- Sarah *is* young for that job.

In the first two examples here, the verb is followed by a noun referring to the same person as the noun that precedes the verb; the first noun ("Sarah") is the subject in both sentences, while the second noun ("President") is the "predicate nominative." In the third sentence, "Sarah" is again the subject, and "young" serves a function similar to that of the predicate nominatives in the first two sentences, but would be called a "predicate adjective," since it describes the subject and is not a noun in its own right.

In formal English, if we need to use a pronoun in the predicate nominative position, we put it in the "nominative" or "subjective" case (I, we, you, he, she, it, they) because the predicate nominative is being identified with the subject. For example,

- Who is there? It is *I*.
- Is the President talking? Yes, it is *she*.

In colloquial English, it is all right to say, "It's me." But in formal English one would avoid that.

Greek is like formal English in this respect. Thus when you see forms of the Greek verbs meaning "be" (εἰμί) and "become" (γίνομαι), you will often find some word in the nominative case serving as a predicate nominative or adjective.

Action verbs can be either transitive or intransitive. When they are *intransitive,* they produce very simple sentences, because the action of the verb does not carry over into any object. It is complete in itself. For example,

- Let's *eat* now.
- Did you *run* this morning?
- They *talk* too much.

In each of these sentences, there is an adverb ("now," "too much") or adverbial expression ("this morning"). Otherwise, the sentence is simply the most basic type possible: a subject and a verb.

When an action verb is *transitive,* however, it carries its action outward onto something and needs at least one *object* to receive the action. For example,

- I *ran* the *race.*
- The wrestler *throws* his *opponent.*
- The instructor *gave directions.*

Here the noun that follows the verb is not the same as the subject. It is not a predicate nominative, as with the linking verbs, but a "direct object," since it receives the action of the verb directly. If we substitute pronouns here, we should have to use our English "accusative" or "objective" case (i.e., me, us, you, him, her, it, them):

- I ran *it.*
- He throws *him.*
- She gave *them.*

A transitive verb can also have another kind of object, indicating the person to or for whom the action occurred or whom the action benefited. This is the "indirect object." In English we often indicate it with the prepositions "to" or "for" — but not always. Sometimes we just throw the word into the sentence in a characteristic place (between the verb and the direct object). Either way, the indirect object is in the objective case. For example,

- I wrote a letter *to him.*
  or
- I wrote *him* a letter.

In both forms of this sentence, "letter" is the direct object and "him" is the indirect object. Another example:

- We did a favor *for her.*
  or
- We did *her* a favor.

Here "favor" is the direct object and "her" is the indirect object.

With transitive verbs, Greek is rather like English, but more precise. Not only pronouns, but also nouns and adjectives must show the proper case for the function they serve. What is more, where we make do with one "objective" case, Greek distinguishes between an accusative case, which most direct objects fall into, and a dative case, used for indirect objects.

The main point to absorb from all this right now is that there are two basic kinds of verbs and that they call for two quite different kinds of sentences. In both English and Greek, the choice is:

Linking verb: subject-verb-predicate nominative
Action verb: subject-verb-indirect object-direct object*

In each case, the substantives (nouns, pronouns, adjectives) associated with the verb must appear in forms consistent with their roles in the sentence. These varying forms are called "cases," and each case has its distinctive function in the sentence. The main Greek cases are:

nominative   used for subjects and predicate nominatives
genitive   used to show possession
dative   used for indirect objects
accusative   used for direct objects

The latter three cases (genitive, dative, and accusative) are often called the "oblique" cases.

EXERCISES

A. Give the person and number of the verbs in the following sentences. Most of the time, in English, only the subject will tell you.

1. We all give to the common fund.
2. But it never gives anything back.
3. Do you people think this is a good idea?
4. I certainly don't.
5. The treasurer will have something to answer for.

B. Over the main grammatical elements of each of the following sentences write the symbol indicating the function of each, i.e.,

* This, of course, is the transitive-verb sentence; the intransitive verb makes for a very simple sentence, basically just subject-verb.

S   subject
V   verb
PN   predicate nominative
PA   predicate adjective
IO   indirect object
DO direct object

I. Linking Verb sentences:

1. Sarah is a student.
2. The Dean of the school is a human being.
3. The professor became a madman.
4. God is love.
5. The sky is becoming cloudy.
6. His hair is red.

II. Action verb sentences (more interesting, of course):

1. The vampire bit her.
2. The angel gave her a letter.
3. They fell into a trap.
4. The terrorists surrendered them to us.
5. We gave them a lecture.

III. Mixed examples:

1. Lucy Mae is Queen of the Universe.
2. She rules the planets.
3. She did the Emperor a favor.
4. He tossed her a sausage.
5. They wrote an epitaph for him.
6. We are her servants.
7. She has the greatest power.
8. Her enemies are rebelling.
9. The rebels will become her slaves.
10. She will lay down rules for them.
11. You will be cooperative,
12. or you will be sorry.
13. We shall all sing her praises.
14. She will give us a smile and a wave.

LESSON III

Always read the Greek aloud a few times to develop ease with it. Then translate as you are able with the help of the notes.

²καὶ ἡ ζωὴ ἐφανερώθη, καὶ ἑωράκαμεν καὶ μαρτυροῦμεν καὶ ἀπαγγέλλομεν ὑμῖν τὴν ζωὴν τὴν αἰώνιον ἥτις ἦν πρὸς τὸν πατέρα καὶ ἐφανερώθη ἡμῖν — ³ὃ ἑωράκαμεν καὶ ἀκηκόαμεν ἀπαγγέλλομεν καὶ ὑμῖν, ἵνα καὶ ὑμεῖς κοινωνίαν ἔχητε μεθ' ἡμῶν.

1:2   καὶ   *and*

ἡ ζωὴ   *the life*   The same phrase appeared at the end of verse 1, but this time it is in the nominative case since it is the subject of the verb that follows.

ἐφανερώθη   *was made manifest, appeared,* a 3rd sg. form

ἑωράκαμεν   as in 1:1

μαρτυροῦμεν   *we testify*   Notice the -μεν ending for 1st pl.

ἀπαγγέλλομεν   *we report, declare*

ὑμῖν   *to you,* dative pl., expressing the indirect object

τὴν ζωὴν   like ἡ ζωὴ above, except now accusative case as direct object of ἀπαγγέλλομεν

14

τὴν αἰώνιον   *eternal,* an adjective that goes with τὴν ζωὴν

ἥτις   *which,* a form of the relative pronoun

ἦν   as in 1:1, an irregular 3rd sg. verbal form

πρὸς τὸν πατέρα   *in the presence of the Father*   Note that Greek uses capitals only rarely. Capitals begin paragraphs or other major divisions and signal proper names; words for God are not usually capitalized.

ἡμῖν   *to us,* dative pl., indirect object of ἐφανερώθη

1:3   ὃ   as in 1:1

ἀκηκόαμεν   as in 1:1

καὶ   The καί after ἀπαγγέλλομεν is not needed as a conjunction ("and"); καί often acts, as here, like an adverb meaning "also" or "even."

ἵνα   *so that*

ὑμεῖς   *you yourselves,* nominative case to emphasize the subject of ἔχητε

κοινωνίαν   *communion, partnership, sharing*

ἔχητε   *you may have*   2nd pl. verb endings are -τε and -σθε.

μεθ' ἡμῶν   short for μετὰ *(with)* ἡμῶν *(us)*   Note how the rough breathing on ἡμῶν has changed the preceding τ to θ (μετ' becomes μεθ').

β' ΓΡΑΜΜΑΤΙΚΑ

A Case of Cases

English has three cases: nominative (or subjective), used for subjects and predicate nominatives, possessive, indicating ownership or other close relationship, and accusative (or objective), used for direct and indirect objects and objects of prepositions. We can see the possessive case in nouns (e.g., "the *child's* toy"), but the other two are distinguished only in pronouns, for example, the first person personal pronouns:

nom. / subj.	I	we
poss.	my	our
acc. / obj.	me	us

Greek has, for the most part, four cases. (Some nouns also have a distinct vocative case, which is used in direct address.) They are *nominative*, used like English nominative, *genitive,* used to show possession and also in a few other ways, *dative,* used for indirect objects and to show the means by which an action is accomplished, and *accusative*, used for direct objects. Genitive, dative, and accusative also function as objects of prepositions — a subject to be taken up in more detail in Lesson V.

As in English, the cases have distinct forms. Here are the Greek personal pronouns for 1st and 2nd persons plural. We have already encountered a number of these forms in our reading:

	1st pl.	2nd pl.
nom.	ἡμεῖς	ὑμεῖς
gen.	ἡμῶν	ὑμῶν
dat.	ἡμῖν	ὑμῖν
acc.	ἡμᾶς	ὑμᾶς

You might wonder why Greek would need a nominative form for these pronouns, since they would hardly be used as predicate nominatives and verbs already contain information about their subjects in the form of the personal endings -μεν, -μεθα ("we") and -τε, -σθε (pl. "you"). The answer is that the nominative forms are used only when one wants to emphasize the subject strongly: *we ourselves, you yourselves.*

Here are some examples of the use of cases drawn from our reading thus far:

1:1 ἑωράκαμεν τοῖς ὀφθαλμοῖς ἡμῶν   *we have seen with our eyes*
Dative τοῖς ὀφθαλμοῖς shows *means;* genitive ἡμῶν shows possession.

περὶ τοῦ λόγου τῆς ζωῆς   *concerning the word of life*
Genitive τοῦ λόγου is the object of the preposition περὶ; genitive

τῆς ζωῆς further defines what λόγος is meant. Very often, as here, a Greek genitive is equivalent to an English prepositional phrase starting with "of."

1:2 ἀπαγγέλλομεν ὑμῖν τὴν ζωὴν τὴν αἰώνιον   *we declare to you eternal life*   Dative ὑμῖν is the indirect object; accusative τὴν ζωὴν τὴν αἰώνιον is the direct object.

ἥτις ἦν πρὸς τὸν πατέρα   *which was in the presence of the Father*   Nominative ἥτις is subject; accusative τὸν πατέρα is the object of the preposition πρός.

1:3 μεθ' ἡμῶν   *with us*   Genitive ἡμῶν is the object of the preposition μεθ' (short for μετά).

Gender and Parsing

Greek nouns all have gender. But gender in Greek is different from gender in English. In English, we claim to use "natural" gender. That is, we use feminine pronouns for female persons and animals, masculine pronouns for male persons and animals, neuter for the rest. Greek use of gender is apt to seem rather arbitrary by our standards. As in English, there are three genders: masculine, feminine, and neuter. But a great many nouns that would be neuter in English are either masculine or feminine in Greek — for example:

ἀρχή	*beginning*	feminine
ὀφθαλμός	*eye*	masculine
χείρ	*hand*	fem.
λόγος	*word*	masc.
ζωή	*life*	fem.
κοινωνία	*communion*	fem.

It is important, for a great variety of reasons, to know the gender of each and every noun. The gender has to be learned along with the word, and from here on it will be part of the information given with each noun in the notes to the readings.*

---

* The list above includes all the nouns that we have encountered in the readings except for πατέρα, "father," which is masculine.

Gender is part of the full description of a noun, along with its case and number. By describing just these three elements, you can specify the exact form of a substantive (noun, pronoun, or adjective). For example, in this lesson's reading, ζωή is feminine nominative singular, ζωήν and the adjective αἰώνιον are both fem. acc. sg., and πατέρα is masc. acc. sg. This exact grammatical description of a word is called "parsing" and is often quite useful for talking about and understanding a text.

The Definite Article

Greek has no indefinite article like English "a, an," and it uses its definite article differently from ours. For example, the Greek definite article is regularly found in front of proper names and abstract nouns (e.g., "life"). Still, on the whole, it is roughly equivalent in meaning to English "the."

This book is designed so that students can avoid, as much as possible, memorizing paradigms (a grammatical "paradigm" is a chart of all the possible forms of a word). But a few paradigms are so useful that they are worth memorizing. The paradigm of the definite article is very useful because it provides a ready key to recognizing case and number in about half of all Greek nouns. Memorize the forms in this paradigm in this order: nominative singular, genitive singular, etc., taking the three genders together each time. Getting this by heart now will save much time and trouble later on.

	sg.			pl.		
	m.	f.	n.	m.	f.	n.
nom.	ὁ	ἡ	τό	οἱ	αἱ	τά
gen.	τοῦ	τῆς	τοῦ	τῶν	τῶν	τῶν
dat.	τῷ	τῇ	τῷ	τοῖς	ταῖς	τοῖς
acc.	τόν	τήν	τό	τούς	τάς	τά

Many of the forms listed here have acute accents, but when you see them in actual texts the accents will almost always be grave rather than acute. In classical Greek, when the acute pitch fell on a final syllable, it almost always changed to grave if another word followed directly. Naturally, there is almost always another word after the article. In fact, you will seldom see an acute accent on the final syllable of any word. Expect

to see an acute accent on the final syllable only directly before a punctuation mark or before a group of little words (called "enclitics") that
surrender their own accent to the preceding word.*

* You would see an acute accent on a form of the article only when it is being cited as
a specific word (e.g., τοῦτο τό, "this [word] τό; τὸ τήν, "the [word] τήν") or when it
is followed by an enclitic (e.g., τούς τε λόγους, "and the words"; τόν τε ὀφθαλμόν,
"and the eye").

LESSON IV

α΄ ΛΕΞΙΣ   1 John 1:3b-5

καὶ ἡ κοινωνία δὲ ἡ ἡμετέρα μετὰ τοῦ πατρὸς καὶ μετὰ τοῦ υἱοῦ αὐτοῦ Ἰησοῦ Χριστοῦ. ⁴καὶ ταῦτα γράφομεν ἡμεῖς ἵνα ἡ χαρὰ ἡμῶν ᾖ πεπληρωμένη.

⁵Καὶ ἔστιν αὕτη ἡ ἀγγελία ἣν ἀκηκόαμεν ἀπ᾽ αὐτοῦ καὶ ἀναγγέλλομεν ὑμῖν, ὅτι ὁ θεὸς φῶς ἐστιν καὶ σκοτία ἐν αὐτῷ οὐκ ἔστιν οὐδεμία.

1:3b καὶ . . . δὲ   *and in fact* . . .   In this combination, δέ is the conjunction and καί is serving its intensive function (see the note on 1:3a in Lesson III). δέ can mean either "and" or "but." It is never the first word in its clause, but its translation does, of course, have to come first in English.

κοινωνία   see note on 1:3a in Lesson III

ἡ ἡμετέρα   "our"   The pronoun ἡμῶν is the more common way of saying "our," but this time "our" is expressed with an adjective rather than the pronoun. The definite article is often used with adjectives as a kind of "glue" to bind the adjectives closely to the nouns that they modify (here the noun is κοινωνία). In these instances the definite article cannot be translated.

μετὰ   "with, along with" when used, as here, with a substantive in the genitive case

πατρὸς   masc. gen. sg. of πατήρ, "father"

20

υἱοῦ   masc. gen. sg. of υἱός, "son"

αὐτοῦ   *of him, his*

Ἰησοῦ Χριστοῦ   masc. gen. sg. of — guess what?   The nominative forms are Ἰησοῦς Χριστός. Note that when a breathing or accent mark is used with a capital letter, it is placed directly before the letter.

1:4   ταῦτα   neut. acc. pl., *these things*

γράφομεν   *we are writing*

ἵνα   see notes on 1:3a in Lesson III

ἡ χαρὰ   fem. nom. sg., *joy*

ᾗ πεπληρωμένη   *may be fulfilled*

1:5   ἔστιν   *is*

αὕτη   fem. nom. sg., *this*

ἀγγελία   fem. nom. sg., *message*

ἣν   fem. acc. sg. of the relative pronoun, *which*

ἀκηκόαμεν   as in 1:1

ἀπ᾽ αὐτοῦ   *from him*   ἀπ᾽ is short for ἀπό, a preposition that takes its object in the genitive. αὐτοῦ is masc. gen. sg. of the 3rd person personal pronoun — same as the word for "his" in v. 3.

ἀναγγέλλομεν   *we report, announce, proclaim*   This verb is similar in meaning to ἀπαγγέλλω (v. 3a), and both are from the same root as ἀγγελία.

ὅτι   *that*: introduces indirect discourse

θεὸς   masc. nom. sg., *god*   When this noun has the article with it, as here, it often means "God," but it can simply mean "the god."

φῶς   neut. nom. sg., *light*

σκοτία   fem. nom. sg., *darkness*

ἐν αὐτῷ   *in him*   The preposition ἐν always takes the dative case for its object.

οὐκ   *not*

οὐδεμία   fem. nom. sg., *none at all*   Note that Greek routinely doubles negatives in a way considered colloquial (or even ill-educated) in English. The fact that this adjective is fem. nom. sg. shows that it goes with the nearest noun of the same description. Which noun is that?

β′ ΓΡΑΜΜΑΤΙΚΑ

The Relative Pronoun *(who, which, that)*

The relative pronoun is used, in Greek as in English, to introduce a subordinate clause that describes some person or thing. For example:

• People *who have learned Greek* are no longer barbarians.
• The Greek language, *which was used by the writers of the New Testament,* is well worth learning.
• The person *who wrote this book* is very pushy about this stuff.
• The book *that he wrote* is fascinating.

The *forms* of the Greek relative pronoun are very similar to those of the definite article. Turn to p. 180 for the paradigm. The main difference is that all forms of the relative pronoun begin with rough breathing while most forms of the definite article begin with the letter tau. A few forms of the article, however, also begin with rough breathing, which can cause confusion. Four forms of the relative pronoun, in fact, are identical to forms of the article with one small exception: The pronoun forms all have accents, which the article forms normally do not have.
Compare:

article		relative pronoun
ὁ (m. nom. sg.)	with	ὅ (n. nom. or acc. sg.)
ἡ (f. nom. sg.)	with	ἥ (f. nom. sg.)
οἱ (m. nom. pl.)	with	οἵ (m. nom. pl.)
αἱ (f. nom. pl.)	with	αἵ (f. nom. pl.)

No form of the definite article without tau ever has an accent unless it is directly followed by an enclitic. Therefore, forms with accents are usually relative pronouns.

Greek uses the relative pronoun in ways broadly similar to English. In English the pronoun agrees with its antecedent (the noun it refers to) in gender. But we have just two genders in our relative pronoun: a "personal" gender ("who," common to masculine and feminine) and a neuter gender ("which" or "that").

Thus:

- The *guy who* wrote this book was a flake.
- The *professor who* is teaching the course now is quite good.
- The *curriculum, which* requires us to take it, is sadistic.
- But the *knowledge that* comes of it will make it all completely worthwhile.

In Greek, as well, the gender of the pronoun is determined by the antecedent. If you see a neuter relative pronoun, for example, look for a neuter antecedent.

Unlike English, Greek also distinguishes singular and plural forms. (In English, "who," "which," and "that" are both singular and plural.) A relative pronoun must agree with its antecedent in number as well as gender. For example, ὁ υἱὸς ὅς ("the son who"), but οἱ υἱοὶ οἵ ("the sons who").

The case of a relative pronoun is determined, in both Greek and English, by the pronoun's relation to the other words in its own clause, not by the case of its antecedent. Is it the object of a verb? Then it must be in the accusative. For example:

- The professor *whom* we have now is a great improvement.

Here the antecedent, "professor," is the subject of "is," but "whom" is the object of "have" and is therefore in the accusative case. But if the relative pronoun shows possession, it must be in the genitive. For example:

- The professor *whose* book we are using just finished writing it.

Here again, though the antecedent is the subject of the main verb, "finished," the relative pronoun has to be in a different case. Then, if the relative pronoun is the subject of the verb in its own clause, it must be in the nominative case, even if its antecedent is not. For example:

- We are going to picket the professor *who* wrote this book.

Here the antecedent, "professor," is the direct object of "picket," but the relative pronoun is nominative, because it is the subject of "wrote."

All this sounds rather complicated — and it might be, if you were learning to *compose* sentences in Greek. But in practice, as you learn to *read* Greek, it will seldom be difficult, since it is sufficiently like how we do things in English. Practically speaking, you need to remember:

1. the distinctive forms of the relative pronoun, especially the few that resemble the definite article,
2. that if you are not sure what the relative pronoun is referring to, you need to look for an antecedent of the same gender and number as the pronoun, and
3. that if you are having trouble figuring out how the relative pronoun relates to other words in its own clause, you need to think about its case and what role you would expect that case to play.

Basic Forms of Nouns: First and Second Declensions

In English, we have two ways of forming nouns: regular and irregular. Regular nouns make their plurals by adding "s" or "es"; plurals of irregular nouns (such as child, woman, man) are formed in other ways.

Greek is a little more consistent. It has three basic patterns of regular nouns, called "declensions." Declensions have nothing to do with the *meanings* of the nouns that belong to them, but they have a great deal to do with their *forms* — and therefore with your ability to recognize them in a text. Fortunately, we have already learned the basic shape of the first two declensions by learning the definite article. The forms of the first declension look very much like the forms of the feminine of the definite article. The forms of second declension nouns resemble the forms of the masculine and neuter of the definite article.

First Declension. Turn to p. 177 and look at the paradigm of ἀρχή. You will see that the basic stem of the word (ἀρχ-) remains the same throughout. The stem is declined (i.e., made to show its full range of cases and numbers) by the addition of endings that are essentially identical to those used in the feminine of the definite article. Other nouns in this declension, like ἀγγελία, on the same page, are different only in that they use α in their singular endings where the definite article uses η. There are even some nouns (e.g., δόξα, *glory*) that use α in the nominative and accusative singular, but η in the genitive and dative:

nom.	δόξα
gen.	δόξης
dat.	δόξῃ
acc.	δόξαν

All first declension nouns use α in their plural endings.

First declension nouns that follow the pattern of the ones we have just looked at are all feminine in gender. There are also masculine nouns in the first declension. They are formed exactly the same as the feminine nouns except in the nominative and genitive singular. Look at the charts for νεανίας and μαθητής, p. 178. Except for the nominative singular in -ας / -ης and the genitive singular in -ου, the forms are like those already seen as forms of the feminine of the definite article.

To avoid confusion, *remember this:* Gender and declension are two different things. *Gender* is a quality assigned by the language to a particular word (or to particular forms of a word, as in the case of the definite article). *Declension* is simply a regular pattern of forming nouns, adjectives, and similar words. The definite article uses first-declension endings to distinguish its feminine gender forms. What is more, many first declension nouns happen to be feminine. But first declension nouns are grouped together only because they share the same α or η endings. They are not inevitably feminine. In fact, many masculine nouns also follow the first declension and are distinguished only by their different nom. and gen. sg. endings.

To know the gender of a noun is important, because gender, not declension, determines how the noun is linked to its modifiers in a sentence. An article, for example, must always agree with its noun in *gender*, even if the result looks a little odd:

	τὴν σκηνήν	*the tent* (fem. 1st declension)
but	τὸν μαθητήν	*the disciple* (masc. 1st decl.)

Second Declension. The endings of nouns of the second declension look, for the most part, like the masculine and neuter forms of the definite article. In gender, second declension nouns may be masculine, feminine, or neuter.

Second declension masculine and feminine nouns follow the forms of the masculine article: See λόγος on p. 178. The only difference from the definite article is that nom. sg. ends in -ος instead of -ο. Here also the principle about gender and forms discussed above holds true, and again sometimes the results may look a little awkward or confusing. Here, for example, is the full paradigm of a feminine second declension noun with its feminine definite article:

ἡ ὁδός	*the road*	αἱ ὁδοί
τῆς ὁδοῦ		τῶν ὁδῶν
τῇ ὁδῷ		ταῖς ὁδοῖς
τὴν ὁδόν		τὰς ὁδούς

Again: Modifiers agree with the *gender* of a noun, not with its declension.

Neuter second declension nouns have forms like the neuter definite article. Study the paradigm of δῶρον, p. 179. The one difference from the forms of the article is that nominative and accusative singular forms end in -ον rather than -ο. It is helpful to note that, in all neuter nouns in Greek, nominative and accusative singular are identical, and nominative and accusative plural are identical. Moreover, in the plural, the vast majority of nominative / accusative forms have the ending -α.

EXERCISES

1. Insert the correct form of the relative pronoun (English will do: use "which," "who," "whose," or "whom" and be excruciatingly correct about it):

- Your cartons, _____ arrived on time, were intact — at first.
- The driver _____ brought them put them on a handtruck.
- Some students, _____ were leaving class, were coming downstairs.
- The one with _____ the driver collided broke a leg.

- The one _____ fell over the cartons smashed the eggs.
- I, _____ am telling you all this, was no part of it.
- You _____ eggs were broken may feel aggrieved.
- The person on _____ they all toppled was even more so.

2. Identify the gender and declension of the following Greek nouns. Use the definite article to help identify gender; the form of the noun is your clue to declension. For example:

ἡ ἀλήθεια   fem., 1st decl.   οἱ βαπτισταί   masc., 1st decl.

τὸ ἱερόν	αἱ δόξαι
ἡ ὁδός	τοῖς μαθηταῖς
ὁ βαπτιστής	τὰ δῶρα
ὁ λόγος	τοὺς τόπους
ἡ εἰρήνη	τῆς ὁδοῦ
ὁ θεός	τὴν γῆν

LESSON V

α' ΛΕΞΙΣ   1 John 1:6-7

⁶'Εὰν εἴπωμεν ὅτι κοινωνίαν ἔχομεν μετ' αὐτοῦ καὶ ἐν τῷ σκότει περιπατῶμεν, ψευδόμεθα καὶ οὐ ποιοῦμεν τὴν ἀλήθειαν· ⁷ἐὰν δὲ ἐν τῷ φωτὶ περιπατῶμεν ὡς αὐτός ἐστιν ἐν τῷ φωτί, κοινωνίαν ἔχομεν μετ' ἀλλήλων καὶ τὸ αἷμα 'Ιησοῦ τοῦ υἱοῦ αὐτοῦ κα-θαρίζει ἡμᾶς ἀπὸ πάσης ἁμαρτίας.

From this point on it will be assumed that you have ready access to the second edition of Bauer's *A Greek-English Lexicon of the New Testament and Other Early Christian Literature.** If you are using a smaller and less comprehensive lexicon or dictionary of New Testament Greek, some of the references to Bauer will not be helpful, but you will still be able to follow the main points of the text.

Nouns are listed in the lexicon by their nominative singular form. For first and second declension nouns, you will be able to figure out the nominative singular forms readily on the basis of whatever form you find in the text. It is not difficult, for example, to connect κοινω-νίαν with its nominative form κοινωνία. For nouns of the third declension, which are formed quite differently from first and second declension nouns, the notes to the readings will give you the lexicon form (i.e., the nominative singular) so that you will be able to find it in the lexicon.

The Bauer lexicon is one of the best tools to help English-speak-

---

* For full publication data see the bibliography in Lesson XXII.

ing people study the New Testament. It contains a great deal of information — more than you want or can use now, but it is worthwhile to learn how to use it from the beginning. Each article in the
lexicon dealing with a noun gives its information in a fixed order,
namely:

- lexicon form (nom. sg.)
- gen. sg. ending (from which you can tell which declension the
  noun belongs to)
- a form of the definite article (which tells you the noun's gender)
- information about the history of the word's usage (in parentheses)
- definitions / translations, printed in italics (in numbered paragraphs, if the word had a wide range of usage)

Knowing this order will help you to identify what you need at the
moment and skip what you do not need. At the moment, you need only
the first three items and a general sense of the range of meanings
associated with the word. Later on, when you are studying a specific
passage closely, Bauer's detailed discussion of meanings will become
valuable.

1:6 ἐάν   *if* This conjunction expresses some doubt or uncertainty
whether the condition could possibly be true and so it requires,
in Greek, a verb in the subjunctive mood.

εἴπωμεν   *we say,* a subjunctive verb   Since we use the subjunctive in English quite differently from the Greek subjunctive,
there is no need to try to translate this verb with an English
subjunctive form.

ὅτι   see 1:5

κοινωνίαν   see Bauer

ἔχομεν   *we have,* from the verb ἔχω

μετ' αὐτοῦ   *with him*   μετ' is short for μετά.

ἐν   *in,* a preposition always taking the dative case for its object

σκότει   neut. dat. sg. of σκότος, 3rd declension; see Bauer

περιπατῶμεν   *we walk,* subjunctive

ψευδόμεθα   *we are lying,* from the verb ψεύδομαι

οὐ   *not* This is the same word as οὐκ in the preceding verse. It appears as οὐ before words beginning with a consonant, as οὐκ before words beginning with a smooth breathing, and as οὐχ before rough breathings.

ποιοῦμεν   *we are doing,* from the verb ποιέω

ἀλήθειαν   see Bauer

1:7   δὲ   *and, but*   δέ is never the first word in its clause (though we have to put our English translation of it in that position). Usually it is the second word, though it sometimes appears later than that.

φωτὶ   neut. dat. sg. of φῶς (3rd declension); see Bauer

ὡς   *as*

αὐτός   *he himself*

ἐστιν   as in 1:5

ἀλλήλων   *one another*   Since this word has a reciprocal sense, it has no nominative case and exists only in the plural.

αἷμα   neut. nom. sg., the lexicon form of this noun; see Bauer

υἱοῦ   see Bauer

αὐτοῦ   *his*

καθαρίζει   *cleanses, purifies,* 3rd sg. pres. tense of καθαρίζω

ἀπὸ   *from,* a preposition always taking its object in the genitive case

πάσης   fem. gen. sg. of πᾶς, *each, every, all*

ἁμαρτίας   see Bauer

β΄ ΓΡΑΜΜΑΤΙΚΑ

Prepositions

Greek, like English, does a lot of important work with prepositions —
little words like "to," "from," "by," and "over" placed before nouns and
pronouns in order to indicate their relationship to other words in the
sentence. The noun or pronoun following the preposition is called the
"object" of the preposition. We have already encountered a number of
Greek prepositions.

Greek prepositions are often grouped, for convenience in learning,
according to the cases of their objects. English has just one objective
case, which we use with all prepositions: "to me," "from him," "by her,"
"over them," etc. In Greek three cases can serve as objects of prepositions: genitive, dative, and accusative. Some prepositions will accept only
one of these cases. Others will take two or even all three, but if they do
so, their meaning usually changes depending on which case appears
with them.

Here is a list of the prepositions we have encountered thus far in
1 John. Review the examples given from the readings. Can you still
translate each one? If not, review the readings.

Governing one case:

ἀπό   with genitive only: *from*

Ὃ ἦν ἀπ’ ἀρχῆς . . .
ἀκηκόαμεν ἀπ’ αὐτοῦ
τὸ αἷμα ’Ιησοῦ . . . καθαρίζει ἡμᾶς ἀπὸ πάσης
    ἁμαρτίας

ἐν   with dative only: *in*

καὶ σκοτία ἐν αὐτῷ οὐκ ἔστιν οὐδεμία
ἐὰν . . . ἐν τῷ σκότει περιπατῶμεν, ψευδόμεθα, ἐὰν
    δὲ ἐν τῷ φωτὶ περιπατῶμεν . . . , κοινωνίαν ἔχομεν

Governing two cases:

μετά   1. with genitive: *with, along with* (to indicate
accompaniment, not means)

ἵνα καὶ ὑμεῖς κοινωνίαν ἔχητε μεθ᾽ ἡμῶν
καὶ ἡ κοινωνία . . . μετὰ τοῦ πατρὸς καὶ μετὰ τοῦ
    υἱοῦ αὐτοῦ
κοινωνίαν ἔχομεν μετ᾽ αὐτοῦ
κοινωνίαν ἔχομεν μετ᾽ ἀλλήλων

2. with accusative: *after*

no examples yet in our readings

περί   1. with genitive: *about, concerning, with regard to*

περὶ τοῦ λόγου τῆς ζωῆς

2. with accusative: *around, about, surrounding*

no examples yet in our readings

Governing three cases:

πρός   1. with genitive: *to the advantage of*

no examples in 1 John, only one occurrence in the
New Testament

2. with dative: *near, in addition to*

no examples in 1 John, rare in the New Testament

3. with accusative: *toward, for, at, near*

τὴν ζωὴν . . . ἥτις ἦν πρὸς τὸν πατέρα

Personal Pronouns

We have encountered personal pronouns for the first and second persons plural ("we," "you"), and Lesson III gave complete paradigms for

them. We have also been encountering in our reading forms of the third person personal pronoun αὐτός, αὐτή, αὐτό. For a full paradigm, turn to p. 185. You will see that the forms are almost identical to those of first and second declension nouns. The only exception is that neuter nom. and acc. sg. ends in -o, like the neuter of the definite article.

This pronoun is equivalent in the singular to English "he," "she," "it," and in the plural to "they." But remember that gender is a *grammatical* property and that it works differently in Greek as compared with English. In English, we consider "truth" to be nonpersonal, therefore neuter; if we want to substitute a pronoun for the word "truth," we use "it": "You will know the *truth*, and *it* will make you free." In Greek, ἀλήθεια is a feminine noun; the pronoun substituted for it will normally be a feminine form, such as αὐτή.

Therefore, not every feminine pronoun in Greek will be translated by "she" or "her" in English. Similarly with masculine pronouns: Sometimes αὐτός means "he," sometimes "it," just as sometimes αὐτή means "she," sometimes "it."

In addition, note that the 3rd person pronoun is used in the nominative only when the writer wants to emphasize the subject very strongly, as is the case with the 1st and 2nd person pronouns, or when it is added to a noun to emphasize it. For example:

αὐτὸς ἔφη.

He himself said [it].

αὐτὴ ἔχει κοινωνίαν μεθ' ἡμῶν.

She herself has communion with us.

Ἰησοῦς αὐτὸς μεθ' ὑμῶν.

May Jesus himself [be] with you.

In the oblique cases, this pronoun, when used by itself, is not emphatic.

τίς ἡ ἀγγελία; ἀκηκόατε αὐτήν;

What is the message? Have you heard it?

ἡ κοινωνία ὑμῶν μετ' αὐτῶν.

Your communion [is] with them.

You can expect to see the third person pronoun frequently. Study it carefully. Note especially that it has a *smooth* breathing and that the accent is always on the *last* syllable. This will help you distinguish it from some similar words later on.

EXERCISES

1. Begin making vocabulary cards for nouns to help you learn and review vocabulary. Include on them lexicon form, genitive form (or at least genitive ending), gender, and range of meanings.

Learn vocabulary as you go; it is cumulative. This is a good time to review all of what we have read so far in 1 John. Many students find it more helpful to memorize whole texts — such as these seven verses — rather than isolated vocabulary items.

2. Try translating the following without looking anything up:

α'   ἀπ' ἀρχῆς ὁ θεός ἐστιν μεθ' ἡμῶν.
β'   ἡ ἀγγελία τοῦ Ἰησοῦ φῶς ἐστιν.
γ'   σκοτία ἐν τῇ κοινωνίᾳ ἡμῶν οὐκ ἔστιν οὐδεμία.

LESSON VI

α′ ΛΕΞΙΣ 1 John 1:8-10

⁸ἐὰν εἴπωμεν ὅτι ἁμαρτίαν οὐκ ἔχομεν, ἑαυτοὺς πλανῶμεν καὶ ἡ ἀλήθεια οὐκ ἔστιν ἐν ἡμῖν. ⁹ἐὰν ὁμολογῶμεν τὰς ἁμαρτίας ἡμῶν, πιστός ἐστιν καὶ δίκαιος ἵνα ἀφῇ ἡμῖν τὰς ἁμαρτίας καὶ καθαρίσῃ ἡμᾶς ἀπὸ πάσης ἀδικίας. ¹⁰ἐὰν εἴπωμεν ὅτι οὐχ ἡμαρτήκαμεν, ψεύστην ποιοῦμεν αὐτὸν καὶ ὁ λόγος αὐτοῦ οὐκ ἔστιν ἐν ἡμῖν.

1:8 ἐὰν   see note on 1:6

εἴπωμεν   see note on 1:6

ἁμαρτίαν   as at the end of 1:7

ἔχομεν   as in 1:6

ἑαυτοὺς   masc. acc. pl.: *ourselves*

πλανῶμεν   *we are deceiving*, from πλανάω

ἀλήθεια   as in 1:6

ἔστιν   *is*

1:9 ὁμολογῶμεν   *we confess*, from ὁμολογέω, subjunctive with ἐὰν

πιστός   an adjective in masc. nom. sg. (the lexicon form); see Bauer

δίκαιος   another adjective in masc. nom. sg.; see Bauer

35

ἵνα   *so that*   This conjunction always calls for a subjunctive verb.

ἀφῇ   *forgives,* 3rd sg. subjunctive of ἀφίημι

καθαρίσῃ   *cleanses,* 3rd sg. subjunctive of καθαρίζω

πάσης   see note on 1:7

ἀδικίας   see Bauer

1:10   ἡμαρτήκαμεν   *we have sinned,* from ἁμαρτάνω

ψεύστην   Look in Bauer for a 1st decl. masc. form like μαθητής.

ποιοῦμεν   *we are making,* from ποιέω

λόγος   see Bauer

β′ ΓΡΑΜΜΑΤΙΚΑ

The Two "Selfs"

English creates a bit of confusion with its use of "self" compounds (myself, yourself, ourselves, etc.). We actually use them for two quite different tasks: intensive and reflexive. Intensive usage reinforces or emphasizes another noun or pronoun that we want to "underline." For example:

- I'll do it myself!
- The Dean herself has said that it has to be done this way.
- You yourselves offered this to us only last month.

Reflexive usage comes into play when we want to show that some person or persons functioning as an object in a sentence is / are the same as the person(s) functioning as subject. For example:

- I cut myself!

"I" am both the subject and the object of the action of cutting.

- The Dean has proclaimed herself Archbishop.
- You certainly gave yourselves a lot of leeway on this project!

For some reason, this dual usage of "self" compounds does not seem awkward in English, but the Greeks would probably have found it a bit confusing. They had two different sets of words for these different usages. We have already noted that they used the nominative of the personal pronouns as intensive pronouns.* Thus, ὁμολογοῦμεν means "we confess," but ἡμεῖς ὁμολογοῦμεν is closer to "we ourselves confess"; πιστός ἐστιν means "he is faithful," but πιστὸς αὐτός ἐστιν means "he himself is faithful."

For reflexives, Greek had a completely different set of pronouns. The most common is the following, used for third person singular ("himself, herself, itself") and for all plurals ("ourselves, yourselves, themselves"):

	sg.			pl.		
gen.	ἑαυτοῦ	ἑαυτῆς	ἑαυτοῦ	ἑαυτῶν	ἑαυτῶν	ἑαυτῶν
dat.	ἑαυτῷ	ἑαυτῇ	ἑαυτῷ	ἑαυτοῖς	ἑαυταῖς	ἑαυτοῖς
acc.	ἑαυτόν	ἑαυτήν	ἑαυτό	ἑαυτούς	ἑαυτάς	ἑαυτά

Notice that there are no nominative forms. Since a reflexive refers back to the subject, it can hardly be used in the nominative. The remaining forms are easy to recognize. Like ἑαυτοῦ, they follow the forms of the oblique cases of αὐτός with a "helper" on the front: ἐμ- for first person singular (ἐμαυτοῦ, "myself"), σε- for second person singular (σεαυτοῦ, "yourself").

The distinction between intensives and reflexives will not be difficult, since we are working only from Greek to English. If you were also working from English to Greek, you would have to stop and think about them a bit more. Still, it is important to know the difference, as it will occasionally clear up a confusion for us.

---

* What did they do for an intensive in the oblique cases? On the whole, they tended to move a direct or indirect object they wanted to emphasize up to the beginning of the sentence, which gave it extra stress.

Agreement

We mentioned this topic briefly in Lesson IV — and even gave an example of agreement in gender (ἡ ὁδός). It is an important topic and deserves a more extended treatment here. The basic principle is this: articles, adjectives, and pronouns that are modifying a noun, either directly or as predicates,* must agree with the noun in *gender, number,* and *case*. This does *not* mean that the endings will always be identical. As we saw in the case of ἡ ὁδός, they may look quite different and even odd together. The essential thing is not that they look alike, but that they carry the same information about gender, number, and case.

The importance of this for the person reading Greek is that Greek uses this information as a principal way of helping you find your way through the sentence and grasp its meaning. In English, our most important indicator of the relationship of words in the sentence is word order. If I rewrite the preceding sentence without regard to standard word order, you may have trouble making sense of it: Important most word order in English is in the sentence of the relationship of words indicator. Greek could and did exercise great flexibility in word order because it had other ways of indicating which words should be associated with which others. "Normal" word order in Greek seems to have been about the same as in English, but you will encounter a great many variations on it, simply because word order was much less important as an indicator of meaning than it is in English.

Agreement of articles and adjectives with their nouns is one of the principal ways of showing relationships in the Greek sentence. We have already seen how the article is declined with a full range of forms accommodating all the possible combinations of gender, number, and case. Adjectives, in Greek, were declined similarly.

Many adjectives, such as πιστός and δίκαιος, which we have met in the reading for this lesson, are made up, like the article, of basic first and second declension forms. The way they are listed in Bauer makes this clear:

- πιστός, ή, όν
- δίκαιος, αία, ον

* The classic terminology speaks of "attributive" and "predicative" modifiers. Attributive modifiers are those that relate directly to the noun ("The *good* book"), and predicative modifiers are those that relate to the noun through a linking verb ("The book is *good*").

All three endings of the nominative singular are given, so that you can see that these adjectives correspond to the standard pattern and can also tell whether to expect the feminine singular to use α or η endings.*

By identifying what words agree with each other, you will be able to unravel apparently complex and confusing phrases. Here are some examples. Try translating them yourself before looking at the translations and explanations that follow.

1. ὁ θεὸς τοῖς δικαίοις πιστός ἐστιν.
2. τὸν λόγον τοῦ θεοῦ τὸν πιστὸν ἀκηκόαμεν.
3. τὸν λόγον τοῦ θεοῦ τοῦ πιστοῦ ἀκηκόαμεν.
4. ὁ θεὸς δίκαιος καὶ ὁ λόγος αὐτοῦ δίκαιος.
5. πιστοί ἐσμεν τῷ δικαίῳ θεῷ.
6. τῷ δικαίῳ ἐσμεν θεῷ πιστοί.

1. God is faithful to the righteous.

Lack of an article before πιστός shows that it is predicative.

2. We have heard the faithful word of God.

The article directly before the adjective here shows that it is to be linked directly with its noun. Since the adjective is in the accusative, it must go with a noun in the accusative.

3. We have heard the word of the faithful God.

Here the adjective is in the genitive and agrees with the genitive noun.

4. God is righteous and his word is righteous.

Here as elsewhere Greek does not really need the linking verb. The presence of the adjective in the nominative and without any article before it is enough to suggest how the sentence works.

---

* Some adjectives use the second declension "masculine" endings as common gender (both masculine and feminine). These are usually less common adjectives or compound adjectives like ἄδικος, -ον, *unjust*. Such endings are called "two-ending" adjectives, as distinct from "three-ending" adjectives, in which masculine and feminine forms are different.

5. We are faithful to the righteous God.

6. We are faithful to the *righteous* God.

Greek does not ordinarily break up the normal sentence order for no good reason. It emphasizes some word by bringing it to the beginning of the sentence.

In reading 1 John, we are dealing with a work written in fairly simple, straightforward Greek, where you will not often encounter sentences that seem terribly contorted by English standards. Still, it is important to practice looking at the endings and thinking in terms of gender, number, and case. There will be moments, even in 1 John, where only these clues will enable you to read the sentence correctly.

EXERCISES

A. Mark the "selfs" in the following as intensive (I) or reflexive (R):

1. The hikers themselves became guides for one another.
2. Each made a route for herself or himself.
3. Some led themselves astray.
4. Others found themselves on the highway.
5. I would never make a mistake like that myself.
6. But the map itself must be wrong, since the Pacific Ocean now seems to be to my east.

B. Correct the following mistakes in agreement, making sure that articles and adjectives agree with the corresponding nouns in gender, number, and case.

ταῖς μαθηταῖς
τῷ δικαίου θεῷ
οἱ υἱὸς πιστός
τὸν ὁδόν
τοὺς ἁμαρτίας

LESSON VII

Beginning with this lesson, the Greek readings will no longer be printed in this textbook. Instead, please turn to the appropriate page in your Greek New Testament. The notes will assume that you are reading from *The Greek New Testament,* third edition (corrected), published by the United Bible Societies (UBS).*

To find your way around in the UBS text you need to know how the New Testament books are named in Greek. Turn to the Table of Contents, and you will find that the first four are named with the preposition κατά and a personal name in the accusative, such as Μαθθαῖον (Matthew); κατά with the accusative means "according to." The phrase τὸ εὐαγγέλιον, "the Gospel," is understood as preceding the names of these four books. The fifth book is Πράξεις Ἀποστόλων, "Acts of Apostles." Then comes a series of letters named for their addressees, e.g., Πρὸς Ῥωμαίους, "[Letter] to Romans." Where there is more than one letter (ἐπιστολή) with the same title, the letters are numbered with Greek numerals: α′, β′, γ′. Then follows a group of letters known by the names of their authors (or putative authors), each in the genitive case, e.g., Ἰακώβου, "[Letter] of James." It is in this group that we find the letter we are reading: Ἰωάννου α′, "First [Letter] of John."† Finally, the New Testament concludes with Ἀποκάλυψις Ἰωάννου, "Revelation of John."

---

* For full publication data see the bibliography in Lesson XXII.

† Ἰωάννης is Greek for "John." Its genitive is Ἰωάννου, and the combination shows that it is a first declension masculine noun.

41

From this point onward, the notes on the readings will assume
that you are familiar with the following items of vocabulary, given here
with brief reminders of their meanings.* They will not be mentioned
again except where they are used in highly unusual ways:

ἀγγελία, -ας, ἡ	*message*
ἀδικία, -ας, ἡ	*injustice, unrighteousness*
αἰώνιος, -ον	(two-ending adjective) *eternal*
ἀλήθεια, -ας, ἡ	*truth*
ἁμαρτία, -ας, ἡ	*sin*
ἀπό	(prep. w. gen.) *from*
ἀρχή, -ῆς, ἡ	*beginning*
αὐτός, -ή, -ό	3d person personal / intensive pronoun
δέ	(conjunction) *and; but*
δίκαιος, -αία, -ον	*just, righteous*
ἐάν	(conjunction with subjunctive verb) *if*
ἐν	(prep. w. dat.) *in*
ζωή, -ῆς, ἡ	*life*
ἡμεῖς	1st person plural personal / intensive pronoun
θεός, -οῦ, ὁ	*god; God*
Ἰησοῦς, -οῦ, ὁ	*Jesus*
ἵνα	(conjunction with subjunctive verb) *so that*
καί	(conjunction) *and; also, even*
κοινωνία, -ας, ἡ	*communion, sharing*
λόγος, -ου, ὁ	*word, speech; reason*
μετά	(prep. w. gen.) *with, along with*
ὁ, ἡ, τό	definite article
ὅς, ἥ, ὅ	relative pronoun
ὅτι	*that* (introducing indirect quotation)
οὐ	*not;* also appears as οὐκ, οὐχ
ὀφθαλμός, -οῦ, ὁ	*eye*
περί	(prep. w. gen.) *concerning, about*
πιστός, -ή, -όν	*faithful*
πρός	(prep. w. acc.) *toward; in the presence of*
σκοτία, -ας, ἡ	*darkness*

---

* If you would like to embark on a more ambitious program of learning New Testament
Greek vocabulary, a convenient resource is Van Voorst's *Building Your New Testament
Greek Vocabulary* (see the bibliography in Lesson XXII). Van Voorst organizes the
material in a convenient way for learning.

υἱός, -οῦ, ὁ   *son*
ὑμεῖς   2nd person plural personal / intensive pronoun
χαρά, -ᾶς, ἡ   *joy*
Χριστός, -οῦ, ὁ   *Christ;* literally *anointed*
ψεύστης, -ου, ὁ   *liar*

2:1 τεχνία   pl. of τεχνίον; see Bauer

μου   gen. of the 1st person sg. personal pronoun: *my*

ταῦτα   *these things*

γράφω   *I am writing*

μή   *not* οὐ is the negative used with ordinary (indicative) verbs. μή is used with other forms, such as the subjunctive, as here.

ἁμάρτητε, ἁμάρτῃ   *sin* (2nd pl.), *sins* (3rd sg.)

τις   *someone*

παράκλητον   see Bauer

ἔχομεν   *we have*

πατέρα   *father,* masc. acc. sg., 3rd declension

2:2 ἱλασμός   see Bauer

ἐστιν   *is*

ἡμετέρων   see Bauer

μόνον   an adverb: *only*

ἀλλά   a conjunction: *but*

ὅλου   an adjective in masc. gen. sg.; see Bauer

κόσμου   see Bauer

2:3 τούτῳ   *this,* dat. sg., either masc. or neut.

γινώσκομεν, ἐγνώκαμεν   two forms of the verb γινώσκω: *we know, we have known*

ἐντολάς   see Bauer

τηρῶμεν   a subjunctive verb: *we are keeping*

β′ ΓΡΑΜΜΑΤΙΚΑ

Personal Pronouns for First and Second Persons Singular

The first and second person singular pronouns are much less common in 1 John than are their plural counterparts. Still, they are important enough in Greek to take a look at, and we encountered one form of the first person singular in today's reading (μου). For the paradigm, turn to p. 184. Note that, for the most part, μ is the "sign" of first person singular and σ of second person singular. The first person oblique forms exist in two-syllable forms for emphasis, but appear most often, as in today's reading, in their short forms.

Forms of the Third Declension

We have already encountered several nouns that do not fit the first and second declension patterns that we have learned. They belong to the other grouping of substantives in Greek, the third or "consonant" declension. For obvious reasons, the first declension is often thought of as the "alpha" declension (though it also sometimes uses η as a kind of "substitute" for α) and the second declension is called the "o" declension. The third declension is different (and sometimes a little more complicated in its formation) because every third declension word's *stem* (for our purposes here that part of the word that precedes any endings) at one time ended with a consonant instead of a vowel, which made the addition of endings a little trickier. In particular, the nominative singular (which, of course, is the lexicon form for any noun) often looks rather different from the stem on which the other cases are formed.

For a good example of a third declension formation, turn to p. 183, and look at the indefinite pronoun τις.* The basic stem of the word is τιν-, and many of the forms can easily be understood as being made up of this basic stem plus an ending. For example, the gen. and dat. sg. forms (identical for all genders) are simply τιν- plus the endings -ος

---

* This indefinite pronoun is identical to the interrogative pronoun, the paradigm of which is immediately adjacent on p. 183, except for the accents. The interrogative pronoun has an unusually strong acute accent, which never changes to grave. The indefinite pronoun has a very weak accent; in fact, it usually surrenders its accent to the preceding word.

and -ι. There are a few forms, however, for which this formula does not quite work. The masculine / feminine nominative singular ending, in this declension — if one could even say there is such an ending — is a sigma. Adding it to the stem τιν- would produce the form τινς, which the Greek ear found unacceptable. Greek will hardly ever allow the sounds of nu and sigma to stand next to each other, so here part of the actual stem of the word has to disappear to make room for the ending. Τινς becomes τις; similarly, in the dative plural, τινσί becomes τισί. By contrast, the neuter nom. and acc. sg. have been produced by shortening the basic stem rather than by adding something to it; they have the diminished form τι.

All this means that there is an element of the unpredictable about third declension substantives. Here is a list of the predictable endings for this declension (those not included are not predictable):

	sg.		pl.	
	m. / f.	**n.**	**m. / f.**	**n.**
nom.	-	-	-ες	-α
gen.	-ος		-ων	
dat.	-ι		-σι	
acc.	-α	-	-ας	-α

There is no difference between masculine and feminine forms; indeed, for half of the forms, there is no difference at all among the genders.

The one real problem with third declension substantives is finding them in the lexicon. When you find a word in a text that you suspect might belong to the third declension, you may have to be a little creative in looking for it in the lexicon. If you do not find it right away, look through all the entries beginning with the relevant grouping of letters. With each substantive, check the genitive form given. By subtracting the genitive ending (-ος), you will find the true stem of the word and so verify if it is the same as what you are looking at in the text. As examples, here are some nouns that we have already encountered in our readings or will encounter in the next few lessons:

- αἱ χεῖρες (1 John 1:1) is easy, since its nom. sg. is χείρ, and the article already confirms that we are looking at a fem. nom. pl. form.
- τὸν πατέρα (1:2; 2:1) and τοῦ πατρὸς (1:3) are a little less clear.

The lexicon form is πατήρ, which belongs to a small group of very common nouns that sometimes lose the vowel from their second syllable. See p. 182 for a full paradigm.

- τῷ φωτὶ (1:7) shows how a basic stem ending in τ often has a lexicon form ending in ς, in this case φῶς. Greek did not like the consonant cluster -τσ- any better than -νσ-.
- τῷ σκότει (1:6) belongs to a common type of neuter noun in the third declension; the lexicon form is σκότος, which looks rather like a first declension masculine, but is not. The stem originally ended in an e-vowel and a kind of w-sound, which later disappeared, leaving the e-vowel to merge with the vowels of the endings. See the paradigm on p. 183.

There are some common third declension nouns that are particularly confusing. (It is always common words that tend to be irregular!) For example, the word for "ear" has the basic stem ὠτ-, which shows up in such forms as ὠτός (gen. sg.) or ὠτί (dat. sg.). You would hardly expect its nominative singular (i.e., its lexicon form) to be οὖς. Not to worry — the notes will let you know about such problems. In the long run, so does the lexicon. It will either give you the basic stem and refer you to the correct lexicon entry or it will show you related words and give you hints about other forms to look under.

EXERCISE

Memorize the forms of τις. They will give you a constant point of reference to help you identify third declension substantives. That, in turn, will not only help you recognize their particular cases and numbers, but will also remind you that you may have to search a little more creatively for their lexicon forms.

LESSON VIII

α' ΛΕΞΙΣ 1 John 2:4-6

2:4 λέγων   *saying*, masc. nom. sg. pres. participle of λέγω   With
the definite article this form means "the one saying" or "the one
who says."

Ἔγνωκα   *I have known*

ἐντολὰς   as in 2:3

μὴ   as in 2:1   Here the negative goes with the following word,
which is a participle.

τηρῶν   masc. nom. sg. pres. participle of τηρέω, *keeping*
This participle is parallel with λέγων: *the one saying . . . and not
keeping. . . .*

ἐστίν, ἔστιν   *is*   The variations in accent on this word do not
affect its meaning.

τούτῳ   dative sg. of οὗτος, *this*   This form can be either masculine *(this person)* or neuter *(this thing)*; only the context determines which is intended.

2:5 ὃς . . . ἂν   The combination of the relative pronoun with the
indefinite particle ἂν makes the pronoun indefinite *(whoever)* and
always takes a subjunctive verb.

τηρῇ   3rd person sg. subjunctive of τηρέω, *keeps*

47

ἀληθῶς   an adverb: *truly,* from the adjective ἀληθής

ἡ ἀγάπη   see Bauer

τετελείωται   3rd sg. perfect of τελειόω, *has been perfected*

γινώσκομεν   1st pl. present of γινώσκω, *we know*

ἐσμεν   *we are*

2:6 μένειν   The present infinitive of μένω, *to remain,* is used here as a kind of indirect discourse. You might translate the phrase as *the one claiming to remain in him.*

ὀφείλει   3rd sg. present of ὀφείλω, *ought*   In Greek as in English it takes an infinitive to complete the idea. Here the infinitive is περιπατεῖν.

καθὼς   a conjunction: *just as*

ἐκεῖνος   a demonstrative pronoun, *that* (sg.), *those* (pl.; cf. p. 180), declined like αὐτός

περιεπάτησεν   a 3rd sg. form of περιπατέω, *walked*   This verb is often used in biblical Greek in the sense of *conduct oneself.*

οὕτως   an adverb: *thus*   The square brackets around the word indicate that the editors were doubtful whether it was an original part of the text here; it may have been added by a copyist.

περιπατεῖν   present active infinitive of περιπατέω, *walk*

β′ ΓΡΑΜΜΑΤΙΚΑ

Indirect Discourse

The words or thoughts of a person can be quoted either directly or indirectly. That is, they can be quoted in the speaker's exact words (direct discourse) or incorporated into the words of the person quoting them (indirect discourse). Some examples:

Direct: She was thinking, "These declensions are fascinating stuff."

Indirect: She was thinking that these declensions were
fascinating stuff.

Direct: I said, "I think I hear my mother calling me."
Indirect: I said that I thought I heard my mother calling me.

Direct: You proclaimed, "Lucy Mae is the Queen
of the Universe."
Indirect: You proclaimed Lucy Mae to be the Queen
of the Universe.

As you can see from these English examples, we have two basic ways of
creating indirect discourse in our language: by using a subordinating
conjunction ("that") to attach the quoted material to the main verb or
by changing the verb of the quoted material to an infinitive (e.g., "to
be"). Usually we use "that"; we use the infinitive only after a few specific
verbs (e.g., claim, proclaim, tell).

Greek, too, has both these systems for indirect discourse and can
use either one quite freely. We have had examples of both in our readings.

1:8 ἐὰν εἴπωμεν ὅτι ἁμαρτίαν
οὐχ ἔχομεν   *if we say that we have no sin*

2:6 ὁ λέγων ἐν αὐτῷ μένειν   *the one claiming to remain
in him*

Sometimes speakers of English have a little trouble with the latter (infinitive) type of indirect discourse in Greek — mainly because it is less
common in our language. Often it is best not to translate the Greek
infinitive with an English infinitive, but to substitute the more usual
English type of indirect discourse: *the one who says that he / she remains
in him*.

One other bit of confusion can arise from an inconsistency in
Greek usage. Most of the time ὅτι functions like "that" and introduces
an indirect quotation. But sometimes it is simply used like quotation
marks and the quotation introduced turns out to be in direct discourse.
For example:

2:4 ὁ λέγων ὅτι Ἔγνωκα αὐτόν   *the one saying, "I know him"*

Modern printing conventions, used in texts like ours, help sort out what is going on. A capital letter is always used at the beginning of a direct quotation, even if it is preceded by ὅτι; if there is no capital, it is an indirect quotation. Since capitals are uncommon in printed Greek texts, a capital in the middle of a sentence often proves to be a clue that a direct quotation is beginning.

Personal Endings of Verbs

We have already noted that Greek verbs have endings that tell you a great deal about the subject of the sentence. This is why Greek does not need subject pronouns, as we do in English. The verb form itself tells you that the subject is "we," or "I," or "they," or whatever. In other words, the verb ending tells you the person (1st, 2nd, or 3rd) and number (sg. or pl.) of the subject. The endings of verbs contain other information, too; but the person and number of the subject are particularly important bits of information — and the first that we will learn to analyze. The chart that follows gives the endings grouped according to persons. They are also classified as "A" and "B" endings. The reasons for this classification will become apparent only later on, but it seems best to lay them out in this way now since it will become an important distinction.

SYNOPSIS OF VERB ENDINGS*

Person	A	B
1sg.	-ω	-μαι
	-α	-μην
	-ν (-ον, -ην, -ειν)	
	-μι	
2sg.	-ς	-η
		-ου
		-ω
		-σαι

* The endings of imperative verb forms are not included in this chart.

3sg.	-ει	-ται	*Similar to*
	-ε(ν)*	-το	*Colwell*
	-η		
	-ῃ		
	-σι		
1pl.	-μεν	-μεθα	
2pl.	-τε	-σθε	
3pl.	-ουσι(ν)*	-νται	
	-ασι(ν)*	-ντο	
	-ωσι(ν)*		
	-ον		
	-αν		
	-σαν		

Some of these endings give failsafe identifications, particularly first and 2nd person pl. Other groupings are very irregular, such as the B endings for 2nd person sg. In a few cases, the same ending can be found in more than one category and is therefore ambiguous. -ω, for example, almost always indicates 1st person sg., but occasionally it will indicate 2nd person sg. The most common confusions are created by -ον, which is a common 3rd person pl. ending that also shows up fairly frequently as a form of the 1st person sg. Context is usually enough to decide which it is at any given moment.

EXERCISES

1. Using the chart above, identify the person, number, and ending type (A or B) of the following verb forms:

| ἀκηκόαμεν | ἔχω |
| ἐθεασάμεθα | ἔλεγον |

---

* The ν in parentheses appears mainly when the following word starts with a vowel and there is a need to separate the two words in pronunciation in order to protect the ending. It is called "nu movable."

τετελείωται	μένεις
λέγῃ	περιεπάτησε(ν)
ἔχητε	ἵστημι
γίνεσθε	βαπτίζονται

2. Translate the following:

α′ ἀκηκόαμεν (cf. 1 John 1:1) τὸν λόγον σου καὶ ἐθεασάμεθα (cf. 1:1) ὅτι ἀληθής ("true") ἐστιν.

β′ λέγουσιν ὅτι ὁ θεὸς σκοτία ἐστιν· ἡμεῖς δὲ λέγομεν ὅτι ὁ θεὸς φῶς.

γ′ γράφω ὑμῖν λόγον τῆς σοφίας.

δ′ ἔχετε τὴν ἀγάπην τοῦ πατρός.

ε′ λέγω ὅτι μένομεν ἐν τῷ θεῷ.

LESSON IX

α′ ΛΕΞΙΣ 1 John 2:7-11

From this point on, a plus sign (+) in the reading notes indicates a word that should be added to your growing vocabulary and that will not be mentioned again in the notes.

2:7 +ἀγαπητοί   a masc. nom. pl. adjective   What would its lexicon form be? (Adjectives are normally listed under their masc. nom. sg. forms.)

+ἐντολὴν   see Bauer

καινὴν   a fem. acc. sg. adjective (see Bauer)   Why is it in this form?

+γράφω   *write*   What does the personal ending tell you about the subject?

+ἀλλ'   short for +ἀλλά   See Bauer and note the accent carefully to distinguish it from ἄλλος, *other*.

παλαιὰν   a fem. sg. acc. adjective (see Bauer)   Do you know any English derivatives?

εἴχετε   *had* (past tense)   What does the personal ending tell you?

ἐστιν   *is*

ἠκούσατε   *heard*   Note the personal ending.

53

2:8 +πάλιν   see Bauer

+ἀληθὲς   neut. nom. sg. of +ἀληθής   This is a 3rd declension adjective that works rather like the declension of σκότος (p. 183). The sg. looks like this:

m. / f.	n.
ἀληθής	ἀληθές
ἀληθοῦς	
ἀληθεῖ	
ἀληθῆ	ἀληθές

παράγεται   from παράγομαι, *pass away*   What does the personal ending tell you?

ὅτι   This little word has more than one meaning; see Bauer.

+φῶς   What genitive form is given in Bauer? What does that form tell you about this noun?

ἀληθινὸν   an adjective in neut. nom. sg.; see Bauer

ἤδη   see Bauer

φαίνει   from φαίνω, *shine*   What is the personal ending?

2:9 λέγων   see note on 2:4

φωτὶ   3rd declension dat. sg. of what noun?

εἶναι   infinitive of εἰμί: *to be*   If the clause seems confusing, review the explanation of indirect discourse, pp. 48-50 above.

+ἀδελφὸν   see Bauer   This is an important Johannine word.

μισῶν   from +μισέω, *hate*   This is a participle, parallel with λέγων above.

ἕως ἄρτι   *up to now*

2:10 ἀγαπῶν   from +ἀγαπάω, *love* (verb, not noun), another participle like the two in v. 9

μένει   from +μένω, *remain*   Note the personal ending.

σκάνδαλον   see Bauer

2:11 μισῶν   as in v. 9

περιπατεῖ   from περιπατέω, *walk*

οἶδεν   from οἶδα, an irregular verb meaning *know*, here a 3rd sg. form with nu movable

ποῦ   see Bauer

ὑπάγει   from ὑπάγω, *go*

ἐτύφλωσεν   a past tense of τυφλόω, *blind* (verb, not adjective) Explain the nu in the ending.

β΄ ΓΡΑΜΜΑΤΙΚΑ

Verb Tenses

Greek, like English, has several different tense forms for its verbs, indicating differences of time and also differences in the type of action being performed. In English, for example, we not only have a present tense to indicate *when* the action occurs, but varying forms of that tense to indicate other qualities of the action. Our present tense may be:

simple:	I read.
continuous:	I am reading.
emphatic:	I do read.

Greek tenses communicate similar kinds of information, but they do it somewhat differently. One result is that the Greek tenses do not match up perfectly with our English tenses. Several of them have peculiar qualities of their own that are sometimes hard to reproduce in English.

The English tenses are

Present	*I look, am looking, do look*
Past	*I looked, was looking, did look*
Future	*I will (shall) look, will be looking*
Present Perfect	*I have looked, have been looking*
Past Perfect	*I had looked, had been looking*
Future Perfect	*I will have looked, will have been looking*

The tenses of Hellenistic Greek (somewhat simplified in comparison with the classical period) were present, imperfect, future, aorist, perfect, and pluperfect (though pluperfect was already rather uncommon). They match up with English roughly as follows:

Greek	English
Present	Present (especially present continuous)
Imperfect	Past continuous
Future	Future
Aorist	Past (simple past) or Present Perfect
Perfect	Present Perfect
Pluperfect	Past Perfect

The biggest difference between Greek and English is that Greek has two distinct past tenses, one (the imperfect) to denote continuous past action ("I *was reading* that book yesterday afternoon"), the other (the aorist) to denote simple past action ("I *read* that book" or "I *have read* that book").

As you might expect, information about Greek tenses is packed right into the verb form itself. In English, we do this only with the past tense: help (present), help*ed* (past). Otherwise, we tend to use auxiliary verbs: *will* help, *have* helped, *had* helped, *will have* helped. The Greek system is more compact. It rarely uses auxiliary verbs. The necessary information is usually contained in the specific form of the basic verb itself.

There are two basic positions where this information can be placed: at the beginning of the verb stem or just before the personal ending (between the stem and the ending). The beginning is easy to find in most cases; we look there for two kinds of tense indicator: "augment" and "reduplication." An augment indicates that we are dealing with a past tense, that is, imperfect, aorist, or pluperfect. A reduplication indicates that we are dealing with a tense of the "perfect system," either perfect or pluperfect.*

---

* A verbal "system" is a group of related forms. The "present system" is made up of present, imperfect, and future tenses, which are all formed in related ways; and the "perfect system" is made up, for similar reasons, of the perfect and pluperfect tenses.

Augments

An **augment** is simply an "enlargement" of the beginning of the verb. If the verb stem begins with a consonant, the augment takes the form of ε:

λεγ-	*say*	ἐλεγ-	*was saying*
μεν-	*stay*	ἐμεν-	*was staying*
γραφ-	*write*	ἐγραφ-	*was writing*

If, however, the verb stem begins with a vowel, the augment is handled by lengthening the vowel, if possible, or, in some cases, turning it into a diphthong:

α, αι, αυ	become	η, ῃ, ηυ
ε, ευ	become	η (or ει), ηυ
ο, οι, ου	become	ω, ῳ, ωυ

Thus, we have forms like these:

ἀγαπ-	*love*	ἠγαπ-	*was loving*
ἀκου-	*hear*	ἠκου-	*heard*
ἐχ-	*have*	εἰχ-	*had*

The one tricky thing about augments is that there are some verbs where it can be a little difficult to figure out where the beginning of the verb stem really is. Greek, like English, could and did make compound verbs. Out of our verb "pass," for example, we have created "bypass"; from "stay," we have made "outstay" and "overstay." Greek does even more of this than English, and this creates a problem with regard to augments. Does the augment belong on the original verb or on the prefixed element? Sometimes, ordinary speakers of Greek were probably a little unsure themselves. But grammar gave a clear answer: The augment belongs on the original verb. This means that when you see a longish word that starts off with one of the common prefixes (most of them are the familiar prepositions that you are already learning), you have to check to see whether there might be an augment buried between the prefix and the verb stem.

For example, in the reading for this lesson, we had three compound verbs: παράγεται, περιπατεῖ, and ὑπάγει. If we separate their prefixes from their basic stems, we get something like this: παρ(α)-αγ-, περι-πατ-, ὑπ(ο)-αγ-. (The vowels in parentheses are portions of the prefix that were dropped because, in these verbs, there was another vowel immediately following.) If we were to add augments, we would get forms starting like this: παρηγ-, περιεπατ-, ὑπηγ-.

For our purposes, there are *four things to remember about augments:* 1. An augment indicates a past tense. 2. When you find a past tense form in a text, you must subtract the augment in order to find the lexicon form of the verb. 3. Sometimes the augment is just a lengthening of a vowel: η will take you back to α or ε; ει goes back to ε; ω goes back to o. 4. In compound verbs, the augment comes between the prefix and the original verb stem.

Reduplication

"Reduplication" is a doubling of the first sound of the original verb stem. If the first sound is a vowel, it is lengthened — with much the same results as if you were augmenting it. Thus, ἀγαπ-, for example, would become ἠγαπ- when reduplicated. If the first letter of the stem is a consonant, however, reduplication doubles the consonant, using -ε- to help sound out the reduplication:

λυ-	reduplicates to	λελυ-
γραφ-	reduplicates to	γεγραφ-
τυφλο-	reduplicates to	τετυφλο-

This is simple and obvious except when the verb stem begins with an aspirated consonant (θ, φ, or χ). These letters were pronounced with a considerable exhalation of breath, and reduplicating them apparently sounded very ugly to the ancient Greeks. Consequently they are reduplicated by their "corresponding" unaspirated consonants. "Correspondence," in this case, has to do with where in the mouth particular consonants are formed. "Labials" are pronounced by placing the lips together, "dentals" with the tongue against the back of the front teeth, "palatals" with the tongue against the sides of the palate. The following table shows the full set of labial, dental, and palatal consonants in Greek (including some information that will be discussed only later in this book). The first two columns interest us here, that is, the unvoiced consonants (those pronounced without the help of the larynx) and the corresponding aspirated ones.

	unvoiced	aspirated	+s	voiced
labial	π	φ	ψ	β
dental	τ	θ	—	δ
palatal	κ	χ	ξ	γ

Thus, a verb form beginning with πεφ- will be found in the lexicon under φ, one beginning with τεθ- under θ, one beginning with κεχ- under χ. The first two letters are simply reduplication, with the corresponding unvoiced consonant being used as the equivalent to the aspirated consonant.

In compound verbs, reduplication, like augment, fits onto the beginning of the original, basic stem — *after* the prefix. Thus, you will see forms like these: ἀπο<u>βέβ</u>ληκεν, ἀπο<u>γεγ</u>ραμμένος, and μετα<u>βέβ</u>ηκα.

Redundancy

Augments and reduplications are not the only clues to identification of tense in the Greek verb. The system is fairly redundant. That is to say, a given verb form in the text — say an aorist verb — will normally incorporate several signals to indicate its tense and other important factors. In the next lesson, we will look at "infixes" — an important group of such elements that fit between the verb stem and the personal ending.

EXERCISES

Put circles around augments and square boxes around reduplications in the following verbs. Where you cannot be sure, you can put a question mark. (In the next lesson, we will introduce other clues that will help you decide.)

ἔμεινα	τέθνηκα	πεφίμωσο	ἠγάπησεν
τετέλεκα	ἔγραψα	περιεπάτει	ἀπῆγον
εἶχον	ἐλελύκειν	ἀποκεκάλυπται	κεχωρισμένος
ἐλέγετε	περιεποίησεν	γέγραφα	ᾠκοδόμησα

LESSON X

2:12 +τεχνία   as in 2:1

ἀφέωνται   *are forgiven* This form is sufficiently irregular that we will not try to decipher its construction here.

+διά   prep. with either genitive *(through)* or accusative, as here *(on account of);* see Bauer for more detail

+ὄνομα   see Bauer What declension is this noun? Cf. p. 182.

2:13 +πατέρες   Cf. p. 182.

ἐγνώκατε   This is a perfect tense form of γινώσκω, but its reduplication is defective.

τὸν ἀπ’ ἀρχῆς   An article with a prepositional phrase is a common construction in ancient Greek. If the article is masc. or fem., it means "the one(s) . . ."; if it is neut., it means "the thing(s). . . ."

+νεανίσκοι   see Bauer

νενικήκατε   The lexicon form is νικάω (see Bauer for meaning). What can you say about the tense?

+πονηρόν   see Bauer

2:14 +παιδία   neut. pl.; see Bauer

60

ἰσχυροί   *strong*

2:15 +Μὴ   see note on 2:1; here, μή is negating an imperative

+κόσμον   see Bauer

μηδὲ   *nor,* a combination of μη and δε

τὰ ἐν τῷ κοσμῷ   cf. note on τὸν ἀπ' ἀρχῆς in 2:13

ἀγαπᾷ   contraction of ἀγαπα-ει, ει being the personal ending

+ἀγάπη   see Bauer

2:16 πᾶν   neut. nom. sg. of πᾶς, *all*

ἐπιθυμία   *desire*

+σαρκὸς   nom. σάρξ; see Bauer

ἀλαζονεία   *boasting*

βίου   see Bauer   Do you recognize any English derivatives? Can you tell from the lexicon how this word differs in meaning from ζωή?

+ἐκ   see Bauer   This word can also take the form ἐξ before vowels.

2:17 παράγεται   see note on 2:8

ποιῶν   participle of ποιέω, *doing,*

θέλημα   see Bauer; this word follows the same declensional pattern as ὄνομα

+εἰς τὸν αἰῶνα   αἰών literally means *age.* This idiom means *forever.*

β' ΓΡΑΜΜΑΤΙΚΑ

More Indicators of Tense

In addition to augments and reduplications, discussed in the previous lesson, there are other important indicators of tense that go along with

them and reinforce identification of forms. This lesson deals with indicators that are inserted between the basic stem of the verb and the
personal endings.

First, a word about the "basic stem." By tradition, verbs are listed
in the lexicon under the first person singular present active indicative
form — equivalent in English to "I am reading." This form can have its
personal ending from either the A or the B endings (cf. p. 50 above),
depending on how the particular verb in question is used. Thus, you
can find entries like γράφω, λέγω, or μένω and entries like γίνομαι or
θεάομαι. In either case you find the stem of the verb by removing the
ending (-ω or -ομαι), which leaves the following stems: γραφ-, λεγ-,
μεν-, γιν-, θεα-. The standard verb used for showing the conjugation
of regular verbs in Greek is λύω *(loosen, untie)*, probably because it most
readily shows the elements that fit between the stem and the personal
endings. These elements are of two kinds: "infixes" and "theme vowels."

An *infix* is a letter or syllable inserted into a verb form that helps
indicate its tense (and sometimes other information).* It comes directly
after the stem. There are four basic infixes: -σ-, which indicates either
future or (with augment) aorist, -κ-, which indicates perfect active, -θ-,
which indicates aorist passive, and -θησ-, which indicates future passive.
Here are examples from λύω:

λύω	present active, *I untie*
λύσω	future active, *I will untie*
ἔλυσα	aorist active, *I untied*
λέλυκα	perfect active, *I have untied*
ἐλύθην	aorist passive, *I was untied*
λυθήσομαι	future passive, *I will be untied*

Notice how the -σ- infix cooperates with the augment to identify the
aorist active; the imperfect (ἔλυον) has an augment, but no infix.

Theme vowels are a kind of glue used in most tenses to connect
the personal endings with what precedes them. They, too, are somewhat
tense specific and help in the identification of tenses. For example,
compare the following forms, all first person plural:

---

* In particular, infixes often indicate something about *voice* (active, middle, or passive)
— a topic we will explain further in Lesson XIII.

λύομεν	present active
ἐλύομεν	imperfect active
λύσομεν	future active
λυθησόμεθα	future passive
ἐλύσαμεν	aorist active
ἐλύθημεν	aorist passive
λελύκαμεν	perfect active
ἐλελύκειμεν	pluperfect active

You could identify these tenses purely on the basis of augments, reduplications, and infixes. But as an added clue, notice that some of the
tenses here prefer an o-vowel before the personal ending (in these
examples -o-), others take -α-; one takes -η-, and one the diphthong
-ει-. This preference in theme vowels is consistent. Aorist and perfect
actives prefer -α- as their theme vowel. Aorist passives take -η-. Pluperfect actives use the diphthong -ει-.*

One group of tenses — present, imperfect, and future — prefers
a characteristic mix of e-vowels and o-vowels; these tenses are often
called "the present system" because they are constructed in related ways.
The e-vowels are used with 3rd sg. and all 2nd person forms. The
o-vowels are used with 3rd pl. and all 1st person forms.

	sg.	pl.
1st	-ω	-ομεν
2nd	-εις	-ετε
3rd	-ει	-ουσι(ν)

It is often hard to separate theme vowels and personal endings
perfectly from each other, since they tend to coalesce. The list of personal
endings on pp. 50-51 is not a "pure" list, but includes some theme
vowels, too.

Analyzing Greek Verbs

Your objective at this point is to learn to recognize Greek verb forms
and sort them roughly into the correct tense categories. You are not
trying to learn how to create the forms yourself — only to *recognize*

---

* Perfect passives use no theme vowel at all.

them. The information presented in Lessons IX and X is presented here in a way that will help with that task.

When you meet a new and unfamiliar verb form in a text, there are seven "slots" to look at. Some of them, in any given verb form, will probably be "empty"; in that case, it helps to notice that they are empty. The slots are as follows (reading from left to right in any given verb form):

1. *prefix* (in compound verbs only)
2. *augment* (in past tenses only)
3. *reduplication* (in perfect and pluperfect only)
4. *stem* (that which tells what basic verb you are dealing with)
5. *infix* (in most forms other than present and imperfect)
6. *theme vowel* (varying by tense and other factors)
7. *personal ending*

This represents a considerable amount of information packed into a very small space. Give yourself time to learn to unpack it. Working through these "slots" is a skill that develops with practice until it gradually becomes second nature. Though it takes more than a one-semester course to achieve real proficiency, you will find that some of it gets under your skin even through the limited amount of reading in the New Testament you are doing in this book. For now, work through each of the seven slots in turn in this way:

1. If the verb begins with something that looks like a preposition (e.g., ἀπ-, ἀφ-, εἰσ-, ἐκ-, ἐξ-, περι-, etc.) or with εὐ-, δυσ-, or συν-,* ask yourself whether it might not be a compound verb. Then check to see if there is anything following the presumed prefix that might be an augment or reduplication.
2. Augment can take two forms, ε- or a lengthening of the initial vowel of the stem; be alert for either. If an augment is present, the form must be in a past tense (imperfect, aorist, or pluperfect).
3. Reduplication can also take two forms, a doubled consonant (with -ε-) or lengthening of the initial vowel. If a reduplication is present, you are dealing with the "perfect system" (i.e., perfect and pluperfect tenses).

* συν was a common preposition in classical Greek meaning "with," but in the Hellenistic era it was generally replaced by μετά.

4. With regard to the stem cf. p. 62. This and the prefix (if any) tell you what the lexicon form of the verb is.

5. Infix helps specify tense (and often voice — e.g., active or passive — as well):

-σ-	future active or aorist active*
-κ-	perfect system active
-θ-	aorist passive
-θησ-	future passive

6. The theme vowel also helps specify the tense:

e / o	present system (present, future, imperfect; the vowel, sometimes combined with the vowel of the ending, can be ε, η, ει, ο, ου, ω)
-α-	aorist or perfect active
-η-	aorist passive
-ει-	pluperfect active
none	perfect passive

7. The personal ending indicates the subject of the verb.

EXERCISES

A. Identify which "slots" are filled in the following verb forms. Since language is never as simple as the grammatical systems invented to describe it, you may run into some problems. Do what you can. Here are three examples:

2 / 4 / 5 / 6 / 7	1 / 3 / 4 / 7	4 / 5 / 6+7
ἐ / λύ / σ / α / μεν	ἀπο / λέ / λυ / μαι	λύ / σ / ουσι
γράφω	μεμένηκα	λύσεις
γίνεται	ἤκουσα	ἔγραψα
ἔχομεν	περιεπάτησεν	ἐλύθημεν
ἐλύετε	ἀπέφυγεν	
μένει	ἐτύφλωσας	

* These tenses also have a middle voice, which uses the -σ- infix.

B. Now go back through the previous list and see what the elements you identified can tell you about the verb. Aim at identifying person, number, tense, and lexicon form. (This is your first try at this. When you find things you cannot figure out, ask the instructor.) For example:

ἐ / λύ / σ / α / μεν	1st person plural aorist of λύω
ἀπο / λέ / λυ / μαι	1st person singular perfect of ἀπολύω
λύ / σ / ουσι	3rd person plural future of λύω

LESSON XI

α′ ΛΕΞΙΣ 1 John 2:18-25

2:18 +ἐσχάτη   see Bauer   The lexicon form of an adjective is given in the masculine gender. Why is the form feminine here? What theological derivative term do you know?

+ὥρα   see Bauer

+ἐστίν   *is,* 3rd person sg. present active indicative

+καθὼς   see Bauer

ἠκούσατε   The lexicon form is +ἀκούω. Can you tell the person, number, and tense from what you have previously learned?

+ἀντίχριστος   You probably do not need to look this one up!

ἔρχεται   The lexicon form is +ἔρχομαι. What are the person, number, and tense?

+νῦν   an adverb: *now*

πολλοὶ   *many*

γεγόνασιν   *have come to be,* 3rd person pl. irregular perfect of γίνομαι

ὅθεν   *whence, from which*

γινώσκομεν   from +γινώσκω   What are the person, number, and tense?

2:19 ἐξῆλθαν   irregular aorist of ἐξέρχομαι: *have come out*

ἦσαν   *were,* 3rd person pl. imperfect indicative of *to be*

εἰ . . . ἦσαν, μεμενείκησαν ἄν   εἰ and ἄν are used here with past tenses to make a "past contrary-to-fact condition." In English, we do this in a quite different way: *If they had been . . . , they would have remained.* What is the tense of μεμενείκησαν?

+γάρ   a conjunction: *for*   Like δέ, this conjunction is usually the second word in its clause and never the first.

+μεθ'   short for μετά before a word beginning with rough breathing

φανερωθῶσιν   a subjunctive verb with ἵνα: *might become apparent / obvious*

εἰσὶν   *are,* 3rd person pl. present indicative of *to be*

πάντες   Look at the paradigm of +πᾶς on p. 184. In the singular this adjective means *all, each, every.* In the plural it means *all.* The word appears several times in different forms in this reading.

2:20 +χρῖσμα   *anointing,* a neuter 3rd declension noun like ὄνομα   Do you see the relation to Χριστός, *anointed?* What English derivatives do you know?

ἔχετε   The lexicon form is +ἔχω. What are the tense, person, and number?

ἁγίου   see Bauer

οἴδατε   an irregular verb: *you know*

2:21 ἔγραψα   This is a form of γράφω. When φ and σ combine, they produce ψ. (Compare the table on p. 59.) Given this information, can you parse the form in the text? A hint: The σ is an infix.

πᾶν   from πᾶς

+ψεῦδος   a neuter 3rd declension noun like σκότος; see Bauer and cf. p. 183.

2:22 Τίς   The strong accent shows that this is not indefinite τις, *some-one*, but interrogative τίς, *who?*

εἰ μὴ   these two words together mean *unless, except*

ἀρνούμενος   present participle of ἀρνέομαι: *denying*

οὗτος   *this*, masc. nom. sg.

2:23 οὐδὲ   *nor* or (as here) *not . . . either*

ὁμολογῶν   present active participle of ὁμολογέω: *confessing, acknowledging*

2:24 ὁ   Note the accent. What is it telling you? (Cf. Lesson IV.)

μενέτω   3rd sg. imperative: *let [it] remain*

μείνῃ   3d sg. subjunctive of μένω to go with ἐὰν

μενεῖτε   future of μένω   What person and number?

2:25 αὕτη   *this*, fem. nom. sg.   Why feminine here?

+ἐπαγγελία   See Bauer and also check the following lexicon entry, which is the related verb, which comes next in the text.

ἐπηγγείλατο   irregular aorist of ἐπαγγέλλομαι

αἰώνιον   see Bauer   This is a "two-ending" adjective. The form here may look masculine, but two-ending adjectives use the same forms for both masculine and feminine.

β′ ΓΡΑΜΜΑΤΙΚΑ

Some Distinctive Adjectives

Turn to p. 184, and study the declension of πᾶς. You will notice that the masculine and neuter genders have third declension forms while the feminine gender has first declension forms. It is almost as if there were two different stems involved: παντ- and πασ-. Since this is a common adjective, it will be worthwhile spending a little time getting to know it, so that both types of forms convey the necessary meaning to you. Also, another important group of words that we will encounter later uses these same basic forms.

Some other common adjectives display similar (but less extensive) peculiarities. We have encountered one in this lesson. Look it up in Bauer: πολύς.* Here, the oddity of the single λ appears only in the masc. and neut. nom. sg. (and also, of course, in the neut. *acc.* sg.). Most forms have λλ. Now that you have encountered this adjective you will understand that οἱ πολλοί means "the many" and naturally will not make the mistake of referring to "*the* hoi polloi" in English. This entitles you to certain feelings of superiority, since it shows that you are a Ἑλληνιστής and no longer belong to hoi polloi (also known as οἱ βάρβαροι).

The Subjunctive

One property of verbs is that they can perform several different tasks, such as narrating action, giving commands, or expressing the subordination of one action to another. Typically, the form of the verb changes in order to indicate which variety of tasks it is performing. This variability in the verb is called "mood." We have already seen several moods of the Greek verb in our texts: imperative (which gives a command), participle (which modifies a substantive or, with the help of the article, functions as a substantive), indicative (the "basic" verb form, the one that makes statements), and subjunctive. So far, your grammatical study has looked only at the indicative forms of the verb. In this lesson, we will take a more careful look at the subjunctive.

The subjunctive mood, in Greek as in English, expresses a certain quality of tentativeness. Its name, "subjunctive," literally means "subjoined." That is, it tends to be used in subordinate situations, not as the main verb of a sentence. It is the quality of tentativeness, of possibility, of the not-yet-accomplished, however, that is most characteristic of it. The English subjunctive (which has nearly ceased to exist in our modern language) shares this quality. In fact, we use it now exclusively (I think) for contrary-to-fact conditions ("If I *were* you, I wouldn't do that") or other statements that are not expected to prove true.

Greek and English do not have much in common in the specific constructions in which they use the subjunctive mood. (As you have seen in 1 John 2:19, Greek uses the indicative, not the subjunctive mood

---

* Another such adjective is μέγας, *big.*

for contrary-to-fact conditions.) All they have in common is the sense that the subjunctive conveys an element of the tentative or uncertain or merely possible. Greek uses this element of the subjunctive primarily in ways that we have already encountered. We have met subjunctive verbs with two specific conjunctions (ἵνα, ἐάν) and with one particular form of the relative pronoun (ὅς ἄν). Each of these has an element of uncertainty or tentativeness about it: ἵνα indicates purpose ("so that") as distinct from accomplished fact, ἐάν ("if") suggests that the speaker may not know whether the statement is true or not, and ὅς ἄν ("whoever, anyone who") indicates that the reference of the relative pronoun is vague in the speaker's mind. Whenever you see any of these three connectives, you should look for a subjunctive verb.

In addition, the subjunctive is used in the first person in a "deliberative" or "cohortative" way — an effort to move people to a decision or an action, e.g., δεηθῶμεν, *Let us pray*. The subjunctive is also used in prohibitions, e.g., μὴ εἰσενέγκῃς ἡμᾶς εἰς πειρασμόν, "Lead us not into temptation."

The subjunctive mood is found, in Hellenistic Greek, in only two tenses, present and aorist. In the present, it is likely to have some sense of continuous or linear action; in the aorist, of single or punctiliar action. For its forms, turn to pp. 186-88. You will see that the active and the aorist passive forms are quite similar to our "A" list of personal endings and the others to our "B" list. The distinctive thing about them all is that they have *long* theme vowels, all of them belonging to the e / o group of theme vowels. Present and aorist forms are identical except that the aorist forms have an infix (-σ- in active and middle voices, -θ- in passive voice). Memorize the subjunctive of the verb "to be" (p. 185), since it gives you a complete list of the "A" subjunctive endings. You will be able to recognize most of the "B" subjunctive endings by analogy.

Notice that the aorist subjunctive differs markedly from the aorists we have already discussed in one respect: It has no augment. Only indicative forms have augments. From this point on, you will need to add a couple of new questions to your verb analysis procedure: If a verb has a long theme vowel of the e / o type, you will need to ask if it is a subjunctive.* If it seems that it might be, check also to see if it has a

---

* If a form looks like a subjunctive, but has a *circumflex* accent over the theme vowel, it may well not be a subjunctive. There are verb forms where two short vowels have contracted into a long one at just this spot. They are discussed below, Lesson XVI.

-σ- or -θ- as an infix, indicating that it is aorist. For the most part, the appropriate conjunctions or form of the relative pronoun will tip you off to expect a subjunctive verb before you see it.

γʹ ΕΞΗΓΗΤΙΚΑ

Beginning with this lesson, we add a new section dedicated to equipping you to use the knowledge of Greek that you are acquiring for purposes of ἐξήγησις, "exegesis," that is, for interpretation of texts. The purpose of exegesis is to draw out the meaning that the author and original audience, broadly described, would be likely to have found there. How might such a text have sounded in the ear (in antiquity, reading always meant reading aloud) of people in the time when it was written? We will never get a perfect answer to that question; but every generation, if it really wants to hear what the ancient writers had to say and not just an echo of its own voice, must undertake anew the quest to "Hellenize," to become Greek enough to understand a little of this ancient language and of the whole alien world that it embodied and interpreted. That is why Greek is essential to New Testament exegesis. It is a door into the world of the text, and knowing it — even a little of it — can open that door at least a crack.

The Textual Apparatus (I)

One thing a knowledge of Greek gives us access to, even if just at the elementary level, is some understanding of the problem of the text itself. Since printing did not appear in Europe until about 1450 C.E., all of our older copies of the New Testament books are manuscripts (abbreviated as "mss."), that is, handwritten books. Because it is virtually impossible to copy an extended text without error, no two mss. of the New Testament are identical. What is more, even our earliest substantial mss. date from about two centuries after the composition of the books involved. So, even in their case, there was plenty of time for errors to creep in.

Since there are thousands of mss. of the Greek New Testament surviving, the labor merely of comparing the mss. with one another is enormous. The modern effort to collect and collate the evidence has been going on for about four hundred years. It is not complete, even so; but it has been possible for text critics (as scholars who do this work are called) to identify the main points where there are serious divergences in the mss. An edition of the Greek New Testament like the one you are using incorporates their judgment as to the best text, the one likely to be closest to what the original author actually wrote or dictated. The scholars are seldom in complete agreement, however, and so they also give us other possible readings in the form of a set of footnotes called the "textual apparatus" or *apparatus criticus.*

On the page of the UBS edition from which you read 1 John 2:18-25 you will find two apparatus ("apparatus" is both singular and plural) at the bottom of the page. The first of these is the textual apparatus; the second is an apparatus of references, quotations, and parallel passages. Look at the textual apparatus, note 2, on v. 20: It offers three different readings. The first, πάντες, is the reading preferred by the editors and incorporated into the text. The second, following the //, is πάντα, which would have to serve as the direct object of οἴδατε not as its subject. What form of πᾶς is this? What would this second reading make the sentence mean? The third option is to have no form of πᾶς at all after οἴδατε. What would that reading mean?

Now look at note 3 in the same apparatus. What alternative readings are offered here? How do they change the meaning of the text? The uncertainty between first and second person plural pronouns seen here is not uncommon in the New Testament letters. One probable reason for the confusion is that in the period when most of our mss. were copied the two words were pronounced exactly the same. Why would this cause confusion?

In the next lesson, we will return to the textual apparatus and begin learning what kinds of evidence are presented there and how to read it. Because it is presented in a very compact way, it may look intimidating at first. But there are certain basic ways of sorting the information out.

EXERCISE

Memorize the subjunctive of εἰμί, *be* (p. 185).

LESSON XII

α′ ΛΕΞΙΣ 1 John 2:26–3:3

2:26 Ταῦτα   neut. acc. (or nom.) pl. of +οὗτος; see the grammatical section of this lesson

πλανώντων   gen. pl. present participle of +πλανάω: *leading astray*

2:27 ἐλάβετε   *you received*

+χρείαν   see Bauer

ἔχετε   from +ἔχω; see Bauer   What are the person, number, and tense?

+διδάσκη   see Bauer   What are the person, number, tense, and mood? Later in this verse, you meet ἐδίδαξεν, which is the irregular aorist of this same verb.

+ὡς   see Bauer   This is an earlier, simpler form of καθώς.

μένετε   This form could be indicative here, but it could also be imperative (see the grammatical section of this lesson). Which do you think fits the context better?

2:28 ἐάν   We are familiar with this conjunction with the meaning *if*. But see section 1.d in Bauer's entry for this word, which refers to this passage.

φανερωθῇ   aorist passive subjunctive of +φανερόω

74

Note in Bauer the separate discussions of the passive voice of this verb.

σχῶμεν   *we may have,* irregular aor. subjunctive of ἔχω after ἵνα

+παρρησίαν   see Bauer

αἰσχυνθῶμεν   aorist passive subjunctive of +αἰσχύνω. What signs verify tense and voice here?

ἀπ'   For the particular use of ἀπό here, see section 2 of Bauer's article on αἰσχύνω. Articles on verbs often tell you about idiomatic uses of prepositions with them.

+παρουσίᾳ   see Bauer   Is this word already familiar to you in a theological context?

2:29   εἰδῆτε   irregular subjunctive of οἶδα, *know*

ποιῶν   present participle, masc. nom. sg. of +ποιέω: *doing*

+δικαιοσύνην   see Bauer

γεγέννηται   from +γεννάω; see Bauer   This is passive voice. What are its tense, person, and number?

3:1   ἴδετε   2nd person pl. imperative: *see*

ποταπὴν   fem. acc. sg. of the interrogative adjective ποταπός, *what sort of . . . ?*

δέδωκεν   3rd sg. perf. act. indicative, *has given*

κληθῶμεν   1st person pl. aor. passive subj., *we are called, we might be called*

+ἐσμέν   *we are*

τοῦτο   neut. acc. sg. of +οὗτος; see the grammatical section of this lesson

+ἔγνω   3rd person sg. of the irregular aor. act. indic. of γινώσκω The full paradigm of these forms looks like this:

	sg.	pl.
1st person	ἔγνων	ἔγνωμεν
2nd person	ἔγνως	ἔγνωτε
3rd person	ἔγνω	ἔγνωσι

3:2   οὔπω   *not yet*

ἐφανερώθη   This is almost identical to φανερωθῇ in 2:28, but here it is indicative rather than subjunctive. What clue tells you this?

ἐσόμεθα   *we shall be,* the fut. tense equivalent of ἐσμέν

οἴδαμεν   *we know*

ὅμοιοι   from ὅμοιος, *like, similar to* The point of comparison (here αὐτῷ) is given in the dative.

ὀψόμεθα   *we will see*

3:3   ἔχων   pres. act. participle, masc. nom. sg., of ἔχω: *having*

ἐλπίδα   a 3rd declension noun; the nom. is +ἐλπίς (see Bauer)

ταύτην   fem. acc. sg. of +οὗτος

ἁγνίζει   see Bauer

+ἐκεῖνος   see Bauer and the grammatical section below

ἁγνός   see Bauer

β′ ΓΡΑΜΜΑΤΙΚΑ

Demonstrative Pronouns

English has two demonstrative pronouns: Our "near" demonstrative is *this* (pl. *these*), and the "far" demonstrative is *that* (pl. *those*). Greek makes the same distinction. The far demonstrative is ἐκεῖνος. It is declined like αὐτός, which means that its neuter nom. and acc. sg. have the form ἐκεῖνο (not ἐκεῖνον). Otherwise, it uses normal first and second declension forms.

The near demonstrative οὗτος is a more complicated matter. Look at p. 180 for a full paradigm. You will see that the endings are just like those of αὐτός, except for the differing accents. There are some irregular and confusing shifts, however, in the stem of the word itself. (Of course, it is precisely such commonly used words, in any language, that are most apt to be irregular.) There are two kinds of variation: First, some forms begin with τ- and some with rough breathing. In this regard, οὗτος follows the pattern set up by the definite article: All forms begin with τ- except masc. and fem. nominatives (sg. and pl.). The other variation is in the diphthong in the stem, which is sometimes -ου- and sometimes -αυ-. This variation appears to be governed by the kind of ending that follows. Forms whose endings include an o-vowel use the o-diphthong; those that have an α or η in the ending use the α-diphthong. You do not need an *exact* knowlege of these variations, since you will not be asked to reproduce these forms in Greek. You simply need to become familiar enough with the forms that they always mean *this* or *these* to you: οὑτ-, αὐτ-, τουτ-, and ταυτ- all mean the same thing.

Imperatives

Here we add yet another "mood" to our study of the verb. We have encountered indicative and subjunctive. The imperative is less common than either the indicative or the subjunctive, but it is still quite common and important.

In English, we use the simplest form of the verb in giving commands: "*Write* this down"; "*Set* it down there, please"; "*Stop!*" Since Greek relies so much on endings, you will not be surprised to learn that it has other ways of telling you when a verb form is imperative. You will find the imperative forms for regular verbs on pp. 186-88. Notice that imperatives occur in both the present and aorist tenses. Insofar as there is any difference between these two tenses of the imperative, it is the difference between continuous action (present tense) and punctiliar action (aorist). The present-tense λῦε can mean "untie" or "go on untying" or "keep untying" (continuous action); the aorist λῦσον can mean "untie" or "start untying" (punctiliar action). With either tense, the simplest translation usually works best.

Unlike English, Greek has distinct third person as well as second person imperatives. Our usual English equivalent is to use "let" as an auxiliary verb: "Let the party begin!" We can also use our regular imperative form, though we usually do so only in fixed phrases, such as:

ἁγιασθήτω τὸ ὄνομά σου   *Hallowed be* your name.
ἐλθέτω ἡ βασιλεία σου   Your kingdom *come.*
γενηθήτω τὸ θέλημά σου   Your will *be done.*

The 2nd person pl. imperative uses the normal 2nd person pl. personal endings. This means that in the present tense you can tell 2nd person pl. imperatives from indicatives only by context. You just have to decide which of the two moods seems to fit a given passage better. We have an example in this lesson's λέξις in 2:27. With the aorist, however, you can tell the difference by remembering that only indicatives have augments:

indicative   ἐλύσατε ἐκεῖνο;   *Have you untied that?*
imperative   λύσατε καὶ τοῦτο.   *Untie this also.*

Participles

Participles constitute yet another mood of the verb, but in some respects they behave more like adjectives. For example:

- "The child *opening* the present was surprised by the jack-in-the-box *popping* up."

Here, "opening" is a participle modifying (i.e., describing) "child" and "popping" is a participle modifying "jack-in-the-box." Participles are still verbs, too; they convey a sense of action and, if they are transitive, can take direct objects. In the example above, "opening" has "present" as its direct object.

English has four kinds of participles created out of two basic forms:

	active*	passive
present	opening†	being opened
perfect	having opened	opened or *having been opened*

---

* "Active" and "passive" voice will be discussed in the next lesson.

† Unfortunately, our present active participle in English has exactly the same form as another mood of our verb, the gerund or verbal noun. You can tell the difference only from the usage in a sentence. Is the word standing on its own as subject or object, or is it modifying another noun? Here are a couple of examples: 1. gerund: *Opening* the package proved difficult; 2. participle: The woman *opening* the package found it difficult. Greek has no gerund.

Our use of these is somewhat restricted by their lack of variety and flexibility, but they are important to our language and familiar to us in daily use.

Greek used its participles much more freely than we do, often as equivalent to a relative clause. We have already seen examples, such as: ὁ λέγων ὅτι Ἔγνωκα αὐτόν, καὶ τὰς ἐντολὰς αὐτοῦ μὴ τηρῶν, ψεύστης ἐστίν: *The one saying "I know him" and not keeping his commandments is a liar.* In this case, the Greek participial phrase might seem more comfortable, in English, as a relative clause: "The one *who says* 'I know him' and does not keep. . . ." But Greek was equally at ease with either mode of expression. This means that we are likely to see more participles in a Greek text than in a comparable English text.

Since participles behave like adjectives, they have to be able to perform all of the adjectival functions. In particular, they have to be able to show agreement with the nouns or other substantives (which are sometimes merely implied) that they are modifying. This means that they have to have a full range of endings to indicate gender, number, and case. In addition, they also have items of verb information to communicate, namely, tense and voice (active or passive).

This means that Greek participles have *many* forms. But all the forms can be reduced to two basic patterns. One of these is very simple: most passive participles simply add the element -μεν- after the infix, theme vowel, or infix + theme vowel of their tense and then follow that up with ordinary 1st and 2nd declension endings. For example, the present passive participle, "being untied":

λυόμενος	λυομένη	λυόμενον
λυομένου	λυομένης	λυομένου
κ.τ.λ.*		

See pp. 188-90 for fuller examples.

Active participles (and aorist passive participles) follow the other pattern. It is a bit more complicated, but we have already learned how it works from the paradigm of the adjective πᾶς. Review that paradigm (p. 184), then compare the present active participle:

---

* κ.τ.λ. is the abbreviation for καὶ τὰ λοιπά, "and the rest," the Greek equivalent of "et cetera," which we abbreviate as "etc."

λύων   λύουσα   λῦον
λύοντος   λυούσης   λύοντος
κ.τ.λ.

You will see that this matches the pattern of πᾶς very well, the masculine and neuter using third declension forms and the feminine using first declension forms.

The meanings of Greek participles, like those of English participles, are determined by their tense and voice. But since we have only present and perfect participles in English, a word about the significance of Greek tenses here may be useful. For practical purposes, you can translate both aorist and perfect participles in Greek with the English perfect participle. The present participle in Greek matches up nicely with our present participle. The future participle in Greek represents that something is on the verge of happening. In all these tenses, the participle does not indicate absolute time; that is the business of the principal verb of the sentence. The participle represents time in *relation* to the main verb:

aorist or perfect	time before the main verb
present	time simultaneous to the main verb
future	time after the main verb

For example:

aorist —   ὁ λύσας αὐτὸ οὐκ ἔγνω τί ἐν αὐτῷ ἐστιν.
            The one *having opened* it did not know what was in it.
            Or,
            The one who had opened it did not know what was in it.

present —   ὁ λύων αὐτὸ οὐκ ἔγνω τί ἐν αὐτῷ ἐστιν.
            The one *opening* it did not know what was in it.
            Or,
            The one who was opening it did not know what was in it.

future —   ὁ λύσων αὐτὸ οὐκ ἔγνω τί ἐν αὐτῷ ἐστιν.
            The one *about to open* it did not know what was in it.
            Or,
            The one who was going to open it did not know what
                was in it.

Most of the participles in 1 John are present active and are used in ways comparable to relative clauses. Other New Testament writers use participles in more complex and imaginative ways than the author(s) of 1 John.

γ′ ΕΞΗΓΗΤΙΚΑ

The Textual Apparatus (II)

There are several different classes of manuscript evidence for the text of the Greek New Testament. The oldest, generally speaking, are also the most recently discovered: They are scraps of *papyrus* (plural, "papyri") recovered over the last hundred years or so from ancient scrap heaps in Egypt. A few of these go as far back as the second century, but many contain only a paragraph or two of text.

The next group, according to age, is the great *uncial* mss., so named because they were often written in fine large script in which, it was jokingly said, every letter weighed an *ounce*. These mss. were usually written on vellum, a fine form of parchment, made from animal skins, which was a longer-lasting material than papyrus. These mss. date from the fourth to the tenth centuries, and the older uncials include the most important and influential Greek biblical manuscripts in existence.

In both papyri and uncials, the script makes no distinction between capital and lowercase letters. Normally, there was no word division, punctuation, accents, or breathing marks either. In about the ninth century, Greek scribes revised their system of writing and introduced all these conveniences, which we take for granted in modern printed Greek texts. Over about a hundred years, this new system of writing, called *minuscule*, replaced the older form of writing. Medieval Greek mss. — by far the largest number of mss. of the Greek New Testament — were written in this new style. These minuscule mss. vary greatly in quality; while some are very important, usually because they are thought to have been based on important (and now lost) older models, others have little value for the text critic.

In addition to copies of the Greek New Testament (or portions thereof, as was often the case), ancient and medieval scribes also made *lectionary* books. In these, the beginning or end of a lesson text was often modified in order to make it an independent unit suitable for reading in church. If one discounts for this, however, their evidence can be useful to the text critic.

As early as the second century, Christians began making translations of their books into languages other than Greek, especially Latin, Syriac, and Coptic. Often these *ancient versions* have interesting things to tell us about the kind of Greek text their translators were working from. While the mss. we have of these versions may not be any older than our Greek mss., the translations themselves were originally based on Greek mss. that were quite early.

Finally, *ancient Christian writers* of the second and subsequent centuries often quote from or allude to the New Testament writings. Their quotations may sometimes tell us something about the biblical text that they were familiar with. We have to be cautious, however, about how we use them. Sometimes the writers quoted from memory or paraphrased. At other times later scribes copying the works of these authors may have "corrected" their New Testament quotations to make them conform to the text the scribe knew.

In the textual apparatus of the UBS *Greek New Testament* the editors tell the reader a great deal about the basis for the textual decisions they made. Skim through pp. xi-xli of their "Introduction" to see what *kinds* of evidence they convey in the apparatus and what *kinds* of symbols and abbreviations they use. Then return to 1 John 2:20 and its textual footnote. What does the symbol {D} at the beginning of the note mean? How many different *classes* of evidence (i.e., papyri, uncials, minuscules, ancient versions, and early church writers) are cited for each of the three variants offered? Which reading has the most authorities cited in its favor? Does that seem to be the decisive issue? What else might be important?

EXERCISE

Turn the italicized participial clauses (or equivalents) in the following sentences into relative clauses, keeping the proper time relation to the main verb:

1. The students *about to take their exam* were anxious.
2. But the examination *having been set by the teacher* proved easy.

3. Everyone *having finished* went out for coffee.
4. Those *drinking coffee* were surprised to find it had gone so quickly.
5. "The professor *setting these exams*," they agreed, "hasn't earned his salary."

LESSON XIII

α′ ΛΕΞΙΣ 1 John 3:4-10

3:4 πᾶς ὁ ποιῶν   cf. 2:29

ἀνομία   *transgression, lawlessness;* cf. νόμος, *law*   Greek uses
ἀ- / ἀν- (called "alpha privative") to negate words. Our English
equivalent is "un-" or the more Latinate "in- / im-." Therefore
ἀνομία is behavior opposed to νόμος, and ἀνόμοιος, *unlike*, is the
opposite of ὅμοιος.

3:5 οἴδατε   We have seen a number of forms of the irregular verb
+οἶδα, *know.* It was originally the perfect tense of a verb meaning
see, but in Hellenistic Greek the perfect tense forms have the
present tense meaning *know.* The indicative, with its perfect tense
endings, is recognizable enough. From this point on only forms
of the verb in other moods or in the pluperfect will be identified
in these notes. Here is the "present" active indicative:

οἶδα	οἴδαμεν
οἶδας	οἴδατε
οἶδε	οἴδασι(ν)

ἄρη   *might take away* (irregular aorist subjunctive of αἴρω)

3:6 +ἁμαρτάνω   see Bauer

ἑώρακεν   the slightly irregular perfect of ὁράω: *has seen;* cf. 1:1

+οὐδέ   *and not, nor* (οὐδὲ . . . οὐδὲ means *neither . . . nor*)

84

ἔγνωκεν   The slightly irregular perfect tense of γινώσκω functions much the same as the present tense since to *have known* something is usually to *know* it.

3:7   +μηδείς   οὐδείς and μηδείς both mean *no one, not one*. Which appears in a sentence depends on the same rule that governs οὐ and μή: οὐδείς is used with indicative verbs, μηδείς with other moods of the verb. Both words are simply the numeral "one" with a negative prefix attached. Accordingly, they follow the declension of the numeral "one," which is as follows:

	m.	f.	n.
nom.	εἷς	μία	ἕν
gen.	ἑνός	μιᾶς	ἑνός
dat.	ἑνί	μιᾷ	ἑνί
acc.	ἕνα	μίαν	ἕν

You can see that this numeral operates a bit like πᾶς, with its masc. and neut. in 3rd declension and its fem. in 1st declension. Be sure to note the breathing and accent marks on εἷς and ἕν, which distinguish them from the prepositions εἰς, *into*, and ἐν, *in*.

πλανάτω   If this form looks a little strange, review the imperative forms studied in the previous lesson.

3:8   +διάβολος   see Bauer   Yes, this is the devil, but notice that in Greek the word tells something specific about the devil's character.

+εἰς   The basic meaning of this preposition is *into*, and it always takes its object in the accusative case. Look briefly, in Bauer, at the range of meanings it can have. Prepositions are often a tricky thing in language study. In this context, εἰς τοῦτο could mean something like "to this purpose."

λύσῃ   Yes, this is our old friend +λύω (what form?). But "untie" does not quite fit as a translation, does it? Check the range of meanings offered in Bauer. Which seems most suitable?

+ἔργον   see Bauer

3:9   γεγεννημένος, γεγέννηται   cf. 2:29.   What mood of the verb is seen in forms ending in -μένος, -μένη, -μένον, κ.τ.λ.? If this form looks unfamiliar, review the grammatical section of the previous lesson.

+σπέρμα   see Bauer and note the full range of meanings

+δύναται   *is able to, can* (lexicon form δύναμαι)   The idea has to be completed with an infinitive, in this case, ἁμαρτάνειν, present active infinitive, *to sin.*

3:10 φανερός Can you guess the meaning of this adjective from knowing the related verb? It is usually wise to check such guesses in the lexicon!

ἐστιν τὰ τέκνα   The verb here is singular and the subject is plural. The ancient Greeks could make mistakes about that, just as we do in our language. In this case, however, the seeming disagreement is actually normal. *Neuter plural subjects,* in Greek, quite regularly have *singular verbs.* In English translation, of course, we have to use a plural verb.

β′ ΓΡΑΜΜΑΤΙΚΑ

Deponent Verbs

In Lesson VIII we surveyed the personal endings of verbs and listed them in two basic groups, which we called the "A" and "B" groups (see the synopsis on pp. 50-51). We have also noted that in the lexicon verbs are normally listed by the first person singular present indicative form, which means that they show either the appropriate "A" ending (-ω) or the equivalent "B" ending (-μαι). Of these two options, the first (using "A" endings) is the more common. Verbs of the other sort, which use "B" endings as their basic set of endings, are called "deponent" verbs to distinguish them from the more standard pattern. This is a useful and important term for reasons that will become apparent further along in this lesson. Remember that a "deponent" is a verb that appears in the lexicon in a form ending in -μαι. It uses "B" endings as its basic endings.

"Voice" in Verbs

We have learned that verbs have a variety of properties: person, number, tense, and mood. There is one final such element to add now to the list: voice. "Voice" has to do with the relation between an action verb and its subject. The subject is either *acting* or *being acted upon* in the way specified by the verb. If the subject is acting, we speak of the verb as being in the "active voice"; if the subject is being acted upon, the verb is in the "passive voice." In English the basic form of the verb is the active voice, and we create passive forms by using the verb "to be" as an auxiliary. "To break" is a present *active* infinitive; its present *passive* equivalent is "to *be* broken." "To have broken" is a perfect active infinitive; its perfect passive equivalent is "to have *been* broken."

English can be a little confusing because we use the verb "to be" as an auxiliary for several purposes. With the active participle, it creates continuous or progressive tense forms, such as "I am counting," "I was counting." When we want to make *passive* forms, we use the passive participle instead of the active participle: "I am counted," "I was counted."

Lesson II indicated that in the normal action-verb sentence the verb carries action from the subject to the direct object. Thus:

	S	Vb	DO	
	The forester	sawed	the limb	from the tree.

It is equally possible to "reverse" the flow of the action by using a passive verb form; this enables the writer to bring that which receives the action to the front of the sentence in order to emphasize it:

	S	Vb		Agent
	The limb	was sawed	from the tree	by the forester.

In this sentence "limb" has become the subject, while the original subject ("the forester") is placed in an agent phrase, telling us by whom the action was in fact done.

Passive voice is said to be one of the last things that children master in learning their original language. It can still cause us some trouble as adults. We use it automatically, without any apparent difficulty; but sometimes when we pause to think about what we are doing, it gives us a moment of uncertainty. For the sake of review, take the following sentences with active verbs and restate the same content with the verbs in passive voice. If you have trouble with the process, pause to identify the subject and object in each sentence; then, make the direct object the subject of your rewritten sentence.

EXERCISE

1. At the garden party, the governess insulted the Queen.
2. The duke hit the governess with a sausage.
3. The duchess tripped the duke with her cane.
4. The servants demanded extra pay for dangerous duty.
5. The Queen issued an edict to execute everyone.
6. Although the pet rhinoceros broke the punchbowl, all had a good time. (Make both verbs passive in your rewritten sentence.)

English has just two voices for its verbs: active and passive. You may already have noticed that Greek has three: active, middle, and passive. Originally, the middle voice had a reflexive quality about it: It was used to express a situation where the subject and object were the same. In most tenses (present, imperfect, perfect, and pluperfect) middle and passive voices have the same form and are distinguished only by context. In two tenses, however, aorist and future, they are different. One might distinguish the three voices thus:

future	active	λύσω	I will untie
	middle	λύσομαι	I will untie myself
	passive	λυθήσομαι	I will be untied
aorist	active	ἔλυσα	I untied
	middle	ἐλυσάμην	I untied myself
	passive	ἐλύθην	I was untied

The Greek verb, as you might expect, typically formed its varying voices by changing the form of the verb, especially its endings, rather than by adding an auxiliary verb.* The normal Greek verb took its basic

---

* The exception is the pluperfect passive, which was formed with the perfect passive participle and the past tense of the verb "to be." E.g., ἦν λελυμένον, "it had been untied."

endings from the "A" list and used the "B" endings to make middle and passive forms. Deponent verbs, of course, had a problem here! They used the "B" endings as their basic endings. For the most part, then, they simply could not form a passive voice.

In practice, the middle voice was not often used in its distinctive sense in Hellenistic Greek. Most middle voice forms that you will be dealing with are deponent verbs that prefer middle forms where they have a choice, that is, in the future and aorist tenses, where middle and passive forms are different. (Which set of forms is followed in those two tenses is simply a matter of standard usage for the particular deponent verb in question.)

You can see from the forms of λύω given just above that the middle and passive voices are distinguished in the future and aorist tenses by infixes. Middle voice forms in these two tenses have a -σ- infix. The aorist passive infix is -θ-, and the infix for future passive is the syllable -θησ-. In addition, the aorist passive has unusual personal endings. Look at p. 188 for the aorist passive indicative endings. Once you have allowed for the distinctive -η- theme vowel, the endings are not so strange as to give much trouble in recognition. But the aorist passive subjunctive uses "A" endings (p. 188). While this may give you an occasional nightmare, most students of Greek do survive their encounter with this bit of apparent craziness.

What does this mean in practice?

1. When you are puzzling out a verb form in a text, *first* consider whether its personal ending seems to belong to the "A" column or the "B" column. If it belongs to the "B" column, check whether the verb is deponent or not. If it is not, then you are dealing with middle or passive voice, and you must translate accordingly.

2. -θ- infix means the verb is aorist passive; -θησ- infix means future passive. -σ- infix with a "B" ending means the verb is future or aorist middle voice.

γ΄ ΕΞΗΓΗΤΙΚΑ

Principles of Text Criticism

Text criticism is a rather specialized art, in which most people (including most New Testament scholars) do not choose to dabble much. If you want to read the New Testament with care, though, it is helpful to have some idea of the process and principles that text critics apply in their effort to resolve conflicts in their manuscript authorities.

The first step in text criticism is simply the *collecting* of variants — and the cross-checking of those collected in the past, since it is easy to get the many little details mixed up in transmission, as easy today as when the mss. were being written. Then there is an effort to determine which manuscripts share some typical variants with one another and so to sort the mss. into "families."*

Then the text critic turns to the problem of trying to *explain* the variants, in the hope that the readings which are more likely to be original can be separated from those more likely to have been introduced later. Broadly speaking, there are two ways for variants to arise: by accident or as a scribe's effort to "improve" the text.

Accidents tend to happen when the eye, ear, or memory is fooled by similar combinations of letters, by similarity of sounds, or by similar phrases. We have already mentioned that in the Byzantine era, the forms of ἡμεῖς and ὑμεῖς were pronounced exactly alike. If a scribe were writing, as was sometimes the case, from dictation, it would be easy to mix them up.

Other problems might arise from the writing system itself. Early Christians habitually abbreviated a number of sacred names, making it relatively easy to misread them. This may explain a confusion at the beginning of Mark's Gospel. Some mss. read: Ἀρχὴ τοῦ εὐαγγελίου Ἰησοῦ Χριστοῦ. Others add two words: υἱοῦ θεοῦ. Ancient uncials would typically have written the fuller version of the phrase, with abbreviations, something like this:

$$\mathrm{APXHTOYEYA\Gamma\Gamma E\Lambda IOY\overline{IY}\overline{X Y}\overline{Y Y}\overline{\Theta Y}}$$

It is easy to imagine a scribe blinking at the wrong moment and omitting the last four letters. On the other hand, we also know that Mark tends to parallel the two titles "Christ" and "Son of God." Could it simply be that a scribe, knowing that, added the second title, either unintentionally because it "said itself" in his mind or intentionally to "help" Mark along a little.

This is a difficult example, since it is a borderline issue that can

---

* For a survey of these efforts, consult Bruce M. Metzger, *A Textual Commentary on the Greek New Testament* (London and New York: United Bible Societies, 1971), xiii-xxiv.

be interpreted in more than one way. A clearer example of deliberate "improvement" of a text appears in Mark 1:2. As most modern English translations note, some mss. refer to the quotation here as coming from "Isaiah the prophet," while others simply mention "the prophets." Strictly speaking, the latter statement is more accurate, since the first bit of the quotation actually comes from Malachi or even Exodus. But that is precisely what makes text critics suspicious of that reading. We have good evidence to show that ancient and medieval scribes were inclined to "correct" their manuscripts — particularly biblical ones. Since they assumed that an inspired author like Mark would not have made an error of this sort — ascribing a mixed quotation to Isaiah — they supposed that they were restoring a more original text that had been corrupted by some fool of a scribe in an earlier generation. In this case, most text critics agree in accepting "Isaiah the prophet" as the correct reading precisely because it is factually erroneous.

We can sum up this discussion by saying that there are two broad rules of thumb that text critics use to sort their way through questions like these:

1. If you can show how a variant could have arisen as an accidental error of eye, ear, or memory, it is probably secondary.
2. If that kind of analysis does not help, you should usually assume that the original text is the *lectio difficilior* — Latin for "the more difficult reading" — not so much "more difficult" for us as "more difficult" for the scribes. We should assume, that is, that they tended to "improve" their texts — from their perspective — and that therefore the reading less congenial to them is likely to be older and more genuine.

Even though this book does not prepare you to do text criticism for yourself, it can help you follow what scholars are saying in commentaries. There are times when variant readings can make a substantial difference in the meaning of a passage. A little knowledge of text criticism can give you, as a user of the UBS text, a special insight into this particular version of the Greek New Testament. An official *Textual Commentary* written by one of the editors of the UBS text gives the reasons for the editors' decisions.* A relatively small knowledge of text criticism will enable you to consult it with profit.

* See previous note.

LESSON XIV

α' ΛΕΞΙΣ 1 John 3:11-18

3:11 αὕτη Note the accent and breathing mark. What is the lexicon form? If you are perplexed, review "Demonstrative Pronouns" in Lesson XII.

ἠκούσατε remember that η can be α with augment

+ἀλλήλους see Bauer Note that the lexicon form is *genitive*. This word has no nominative forms. Do you know any English derivatives?*

3:12 ἔσφαξεν See Bauer under σφάζω. The beginning of the entry should help you figure out what tense this form is.

χάριν τίνος χάριν is a preposition with gen.: *for the sake of*; τίνος is the interrogative pronoun (cf. p. 183)

ἦν as noted above, p. 86, neuter plural subjects usually take singular verbs

τά Use of the article in this way, without a noun, often means that some earlier noun is being repeated implicitly. Is there a neuter plural noun in the preceding clause that τά might be echoing here?

3:13 +θαυμάζετε see Bauer The use of μή here as negative shows that the verb form is to be understood as imperative, not indicative.

* "Parallel," "allele."

92

3:14 μεταβεβήκαμεν   *we have crossed over,* irregular perfect of μετα-βαίνω

+θάνατος   see Bauer

ἀγαπῶμεν   indicative, not subjunctive, since it follows ὅτι

3:15 ἀνθρωποκτόνος   see Bauer

μένουσαν   The verb here should be familiar. If this form seems odd, look at p. 188. Is there a feminine noun for it to modify?

3:16 +ὑπὲρ   see Bauer   Note that ὑπέρ is being used here with genitive, which narrows down how much of the article in Bauer you need to scan.

+ψυχὴν   see Bauer

ἔθηκεν   *laid down*

+ὀφείλομεν   see Bauer   The basic meaning of this verb, *ought,* requires an infinitive to complete it — in this case, θεῖναι, *to lay down.*

3:17 +ὅς . . . ἂν   see above, Lesson XI, p. 71

+βίον   see Bauer   How does this word differ from ζωή?

+θεωρῇ   see Bauer; you encountered this word earlier in 1:1.

+χρείαν   see Bauer

ἔχοντα   if the form is perplexing, see p. 188

κλείσῃ   see Bauer, especially part 2 of the entry

+σπλάγχνα   What is the most basic meaning of this word? How does this compare with modern English use of body parts as metaphorical for feelings?

+πῶς   an interrogative adverb; see Bauer

3:18 ἀγαπῶμεν   here this form is subjunctive, used deliberatively: "let us . . . love"

+γλώσσῃ   see Bauer and note the wide range of meanings

β′ ΓΡΑΜΜΑΤΙΚΑ

First and Second Aorists

As far as *meaning* goes, there is only one aorist tense. There are two ways, however, of *forming* this tense. "Regular" verbs such as λύω use the "first aorist" forms. We have already become familiar with most of these forms (see the summary on pp. 186-88). They involve a -σ- infix and -α- theme vowel in the active and middle voices (e.g., ἔλυσα, ἐλυσάμην, λύσασα, λυσάμενος) and a -θ- infix and -η- theme vowel in the passive voice (e.g., ἐλύθην; in the participle the theme vowel is -ε-, e.g., λυθεῖσα, λυθέν). There is an augment in the indicative mood.

The "second aorist" (sometimes called "strong aorist") is found in irregular verbs (of which more will be said below). The 2nd aorist is irregular in the sense that you usually cannot predict the aorist of the verb on the basis of the verb's lexicon form (which is, of course, present tense). But once you know the basic stem of the 2nd aorist in a specific verb, the individual forms follow a regular pattern, which closely follows elements of the imperfect and present tenses. Take as an example the aorist of ἔχω *(have)*. You could not predict that 1st person sg. aorist active indicative would be ἔσχον, but once you know that, you can be sure that its aorist *indicative* will be conjugated regularly — in fact, exactly like a normal imperfect (cf. p. 186):*

ἔσχον	ἔσχομεν
ἔσχες	ἔσχετε
ἔσχε(ν)	ἔσχον

The *subjunctive* drops the augment and uses normal subjunctive endings:

---

* The imperfect of ἔχω can be distinguished from the second aorist because it is formed on the basis of the present stem, with augment and typical imperfect endings: εἶχον, εἶχες, εἶχε(ν), κ.τ.λ. Second aorists always have a distinctively different stem, sometimes from a root quite unrelated to that of the present tense. This distinguishes the second aorist from the imperfect of the same verb.

σχῶ	σχῶμεν
σχῇς	σχῆτε
σχῇ	σχῶσι(ν)

The *participle* follows present tense patterns: σχών, σχοῦσα, σχόν (only the accent is different from a present participle).

The passive voice also has a way of forming a second aorist, but there is less difference here from the first aorist. The phrase "second aorist" in connection with the passive voice simply means that the -θ- infix is omitted, perhaps because it conflicted with a neighboring consonant. For example, the aorist passive of γράφω is ἐγράφην, ἐγράφης, ἐγράφη, κ.τ.λ.

In summary: The second (or "strong") aorist is an alternative way of forming the aorist tense. It does not differ in meaning. Normally, a verb forms its aorist in one way *or* the other. Very few verbs have both types of aorist. Your only challenge in your introductory course is to learn that these forms are aorists, even if they look more like imperfects. They can only be learned, verb by verb, as irregularities.

Irregular Verbs

The English verb has three "principal parts," that is, three forms from which we can predict any other form of the verb. The three principal parts are present, past, and past participle. An irregular verb is one whose conjugation contains some unpredictable elements, that is, for which one principal part is not predictable from another principal part. We have a number of such verbs in English, for example, "swim." Its past tense is "swam," and its past participle is "swum." Perhaps the most irregular verb in English (apart from "be," which seems to be irregular in most languages) is "go." What is its past tense? What is the past participle? Is there any relation at all between "go" and "went" — other than the arbitrary insistence of the English language that they belong together?

Greek also has many irregular verbs. It should come as no surprise that it is typically the most common verbs that are most irregular. And since the conjugation of the Greek verb is more detailed and complex than ours, there are more opportunities for irregularity.

The Greek verb has six principal parts: the 1st person sg. active indicative forms in the present, future, aorist, and perfect tenses and the

1st person sg. passive indicative in the perfect and aorist tenses. With a
regular verb, such as λύω, one can predict the other five principal parts
from the present active indicative: All that is necessary is to apply the
appropriate augments, reduplications, infixes, etc. Thus:

present active	λύω
future active	λύσω
aorist active	ἔλυσα
perfect active	λέλυκα
perfect passive	λέλυμαι
aorist passive	ἐλύθην

Just so, in English, the regular verb has predictable principal parts: If
you know "untie," you can predict the past (untied) and past participle
(untied). With irregular verbs, you simply have to learn what goes with
what.

The chart on pp. 196-97 lists the principal parts of the irregular
verbs that are most important for reading the New Testament. The verbs
that you have already encountered that appear in the chart are ἀγγέλλω,
ἀκούω, βαίνω, γίνομαι, γράφω, ἔρχομαι, ἔχω, μένω, and ὁράω, though
some of these you have seen only in the form of compound verbs, such
as ἀπαγγέλλω or μεταβαίνω. In the long run memorization of the
principal parts of these nine verbs will be repaid in easier reading of
Greek. But the goal is not so much to be able to recite all the principal
parts of these verbs as to establish in your mind, for example, that ἦλθον
is a form of ἔρχομαι and βέβηκα is a form of βαίνω. In any case, study
these verbs thoroughly; see what, if any, "regularities" you can find and
which forms might be relatively easy to trace back to the lexicon form
(i.e., present tense). The notes on future readings will continue to refer
you to the chart, and Bauer's lexicon will also usually help you find the
correct entry. For example, if you look up ἦλθον in Bauer, it will refer
you to ἔρχομαι. But as time goes on you will not want to take the time
for that with the most frequently occurring verbs. So some memorization will be repaid.

γ′ ΕΞΗΓΗΤΙΚΑ

The Punctuation Apparatus

The oldest Greek manuscripts (the papyri and the uncials) had little or
no punctuation. Punctuation was introduced mostly in the Byzantine
period with the minuscule type of writing. For the most part, editors
agree fairly well with one another on issues of punctuation. You can
usually tell where one sentence ends and another begins in Greek.
Occasionally, however, there can be some uncertainty. In such cases, the
editors of the UBS *Greek New Testament* have supplied a punctuation
apparatus, directly below the textual apparatus on the page, to explain
what the options are and how the editors of other major editions and
of various modern translations have decided the question. Turn to the
explanation of this apparatus on pp. xli-xlv of *The Greek New Testament*
and read it for a description of the terms and symbols being used.

   Then turn, for an instance of the apparatus itself, to p. 817. On
this page there are two points at issue. The first, in 1 John 2:27, has to
do with how the verse should be divided into clauses. The varieties of
punctuation make some difference as to where the emphasis falls in the
verse, but otherwise do not affect the meaning much. For example, here
are translations for the first two alternatives offered:

> And as for you, the anointing that you received from him remains
> in you, and you have no need that anyone teach you. But as his
> anointing teaches you about all things and is true and is not a lie,
> even as it has taught you, remain in him (*or* it).

> And as for you, the anointing that you received from him remains
> in you, and you have no need that anyone teach you; but as his
> anointing teaches you about all things, it is indeed (καὶ) true and
> is not a lie. And just as it has taught you, remain in him (*or* it).

The difference may not be great, but in the first case, emphasis falls
more on the injunction to "remain," whereas in the second it falls more
on the description of the community as fully provided for with regard
to teaching.

   The second item in the punctuation apparatus on the same page

is more critical. The actual meaning of 3:2 may depend partly on how
we punctuate the text. The punctuation in the main body of the edition
represents the decision of the editors and can be translated in this
manner:

> Beloved, now we are children of God, and it has not yet become
> apparent what we will be. We know that when he appears, we will
> be like him, because we will see him as he is.

The second alternative can be translated:

> Beloved, now we are children of God, and he has not yet appeared.
> What we will be we know, because when he appears we will be
> like him, because we will see him as he is.

For the third alternative, look at how the RSV translates this verse. What
has happened in this translation? Does it seem to you to be a legitimate
translation of the Greek text before you?

Now look at the punctuation apparatus for today's λέξις. What
difference does it make whether one puts just a period or a paragraph
division between vv. 12 and 13?

The punctuation apparatus has no ancient "authority." But sometimes it has the virtue of making the reader think: "What is this text
really about?" That is the single most important function of exegesis,
which means that this apparatus is sometimes a very good tool for
exegetical work.

LESSON XV

α' ΛΕΞΙΣ   1 John 3:19-24

3:19 +γνωσόμεθα   see γινώσκω in the chart of irregular verbs
Note that this verb is middle deponent in the future tense, but not
in any other tense.

ἔμπροσθεν   see Bauer under 2.d   An "improper preposition"
is simply an adverb that has come to be used as a preposition.
Such prepositions always take their objects in the genitive case.

πείσομεν   See Bauer under πείθω (watch out for the accent!) and
look carefully at the first paragraph of the article. How can you
tell what tense this form is?

+καρδίαν   see Bauer   What English derivatives do you know?
It may seem strange, but it is not unusual, to see the singular of
this noun with a plural genitive (here ἡμῶν).

3:20 καταγινώσκῃ   see Bauer

ὅτι   The repetition of this word does not seem necessary. Leave
it out in English translation.

+μείζων   *greater*, comparative of μέγας, *great*   In English, we
specify the object being compared with the conjunction "than."
Greek can use either the conjunction ἤ or, as here, the genitive
case: μείζων . . . τῆς καρδίας ἡμῶν, *greater than our heart.*

γινώσκει   Note the paronomasia (i.e., word-play) with καταγινώσκῃ.

3:22   ὃ ἐὰν   = ὃ ἂν, *whatever;* ἐάν can serve as an alternative to ἂν

αἰτῶμεν   present subjunctive of αἰτέω; see Bauer

+λαμβάνομεν   see Bauer   This is a very irregular verb, but
since this is a present tense form, it should not be hard to find.
Check the irregular verb list for a summary of its principal parts.

+τηροῦμεν   present indicative of τηρέω; see Bauer

ἀρεστὰ   an adjective; see Bauer under the masc. nom. sg. form

ἐνώπιον   see Bauer

3:23   αὕτη   note accent and breathing mark: this is not αὐτή

+πιστεύσωμεν   see Bauer under πιστεύω   What tense and
mood is this form? This verb often takes an object in the dative
as the rough equivalent of English *believe in.*

ἔδωκεν   *gave;* 3rd sg. aor. act. indic. of δίδωμι (see the grammatical discussion below)

3:24   +πνεύματος   see Bauer; this noun follows the same pattern as
ὄνομα (cf. p. 182)

 οὗ   Strictly speaking this relative pronoun ought to be in the
accusative, since it is the direct object of ἔδωκεν. It is quite common, though, in ancient Greek for an accusative relative pronoun
to be "attracted" into the case of its antecedent (here, πνεύματος)
when the antecedent is genitive (as here) or dative.

[handwritten margin notes: "(=ου)" and "ATTRACTION"]

β′ ΓΡΑΜΜΑΤΙΚΑ

Comparison of Adjectives

In Greek, as in English, adjectives can be used to make comparisons,
and they change their forms for this purpose. In English, we have two
"degrees" of comparison: "comparative," which compares an object or

person with one other, and "superlative," which compares an object or person with a larger field of like objects or persons. We form our degrees of comparison thus:

positive	comparative	superlative
large	larger	largest
careful	more careful	most careful

There is no difference of meaning between the two ways of "comparing the adjective"; the distinction is purely formal, depending mainly on whether the adjective has one or more syllables.

Greek also has both comparative and superlative degrees of comparison. Turn to p. 185 for a brief presentation of their forms. Most comparative and superlative forms behave like 1st and 2nd declension adjectives (e.g., πιστότερος, πιστότατος, κάκιστος). Comparatives ending in -ων or -ιων, however, follow the third declension pattern (κακίων, gen. κακίονος; μείζων, gen. μείζονος).

In Greek, as in Engish, some of the most common adjectives have irregular comparative and superlative forms. In English, for example, we have "good, better, best" and "bad, worse, worst." In Greek you have already encountered, in this lesson, μείζων, *greater,* as the comparative of μέγας, *great.* In general, the lexicon can be expected to guide you to the correct positive form when you encounter an irregular comparative or superlative.

Both comparative and superlative adjectives are often used to make explicit comparisons. When we do this in English, we use "than" with the comparative and "of" with the superlative to specify the referent of the comparison:

Comparative: This box is *larger than* that one.

Superlative: This box is the *largest of* all those under the tree.

Greek uses the genitive in rather the same way that we use the "of" construction, but it can use it with comparative as well as superlative. We have already encountered it with the comparative:

μείζων ἐστὶν ὁ θεὸς τῆς καρδίας ἡμῶν

God is greater than our heart

An alternative way of specifying the comparison in Greek is to use the conjunction ἤ. In the next lesson, we will meet this statement:

μείζων ἐστὶν ὁ ἐν ὑμῖν ἢ ὁ ἐν τῷ κόσμῳ

The one [who is] in you is greater than the one [who is] in the world

In the Greek of the Hellenistic Age, the superlative forms were beginning to disappear. Sometimes you will encounter comparative forms where superlatives would seem to be more appropriate. In spoken English, the opposite process seems to be at work, and the comparative is disappearing.

MI-Verbs

The great majority of Greek verbs fit the basic patterns that we have already studied. They are called "O verbs" because of the 1st person sg. ending in our column of "A" endings. There was also a small group of rather common verbs in ancient Greek that followed an older pattern of conjugation, called the "MI conjugation." We have already encountered a few chance forms of some of them: ἀφῇ (1 John 1:9) and ἀφέωνται (2:12) from ἀφίημι, δέδωκεν (3:1) and ἔδωκεν (3:23) from δίδωμι, and ἔθηκεν and θεῖναι (both in 3:16) from τίθημι. In some respects, these verbs are very close to the O-verbs. In most of their tenses, in fact, there is no difference. Only in the present, imperfect, and aorist do we find anything unusual or surprising.

These verbs have, basically, very simple, short stems such as δο-, θε-, and ἑ-. In the present and imperfect tenses they add to the beginning of these stems a reduplication with -ι- (not -ε- as in the perfect tense), and in singular present indicative forms they also lengthen the vowel of the stem. Thus

the stem	δο-	becomes	διδω-	so that the lexicon form is	δίδωμι
	θε-		τιθη-		τίθημι
	ἑ-		ἱη-		ἵημι*

In addition, there are a few endings peculiar to these verbs. The two

---

* This verb appears in the New Testament only in the compounded form ἀφίημι.

that are hardest to recognize on the basis of your knowledge of the
O-verb are — as you might guess — the two most common: first and
third persons singular active, which are -μι and -σι, respectively. Thus:

δίδωμι   *I give*
δίδωσι   *he, she, it gives*

For a survey of the distinctive forms of δίδωμι, turn to pp. 194-95.
Look for what seems unlike the O-verb. Other than the -ι- reduplication
in the present and imperfect tenses, the main difference is in the aorist
active indicative, which uses -κ- rather than -σ- as the infix.

In summary, you should learn to recognize -μι as a 1st person sg.
ending and -σι as a 3rd person sg. ending. If you encounter difficulty
in finding the lexicon form of a verb that has a short or confusing stem
(particularly one that includes one of the following elements: δο / δω,
θε / θη, στα / στη, ἑ / ἡ), try looking them up with -ι- reduplication:
δίδωμι, τίθημι, ἵστημι (especially the compound ἀνίστημι), ἵημι (i.e.,
the compound ἀφίημι).

γ΄ ΕΞΗΓΗΤΙΚΑ

Cross References

You may have noticed that there is yet a third apparatus at the bottom of
the page in the UBS *Greek New Testament*. This is an apparatus of cross
references. It contains several kinds of material, all of it potentially useful
for exegesis. One thing found in this apparatus is the source of Scripture
quotations. (We are apt to call these "Old Testament" quotations, but, of
course, first-century Christians did not think in those terms — what is
quoted is simply "*the* Scriptures.") The UBS text also has, in the back, some
indexes of this material, so that you can readily find all the quotations of,
for example, Deuteronomy in the New Testament. Conversely, you can
find exactly which Scriptures are quoted by the particular New Testament
writer you are studying. Turn to the index following New Testament order
and look under "1 John" (p. 903). What do you find? What might that tell
you about the author(s) of 1 John, about their understanding of their faith
and its sources, and about their own sources of authority?

Other citations in the apparatus of cross references guide you to passages that show a similar use of language. Turn back, for example, to 1 John 2:22, read the verse, and check the cross references. What do they tell you about the language in this verse? Do these cross references help you to define or clarify the meaning of the term ἀντίχριστος in the Johannine literature?

Yet other cross references point to similarities or relationships of ideas where vocabulary may not be identical. Go to 1 John 3:22-23 and check the cross references given there. What kind of contact with the Synoptic traditions might the cross references for v. 22 suggest? Notice that the cross references for v. 23 refer entirely to the Gospel of John, suggesting that this material is distinctively Johannine. What is, in fact, so distinctive about it? How does it differ from the Synoptic love commandment?

These brief exercises are illustrations of the ways in which the cross references can help you in the task of understanding a particular text better. But of course the apparatus is not perfect or exhaustive. You may notice relationships among texts that are not mentioned. Still the apparatus is a good place to start the process of placing a particular text in its larger world, particularly in the context of Scripture.

LESSON XVI

α′ ΛΕΞΙΣ 1 John 4:1-6

4:1   δοκιμάζετε   see Bauer   πιστεύετε must be imperative because of μή, so δοκιμάζετε must also be imperative because of the parallelism.

+εἰ   see Bauer s.v. IV.2

ἐστιν   Remember that a neuter plural subject can (and usually does) take a singular verb.

ψευδοπροφῆται   Can you figure out the meaning before you look it up?

ἐξεληλύθασιν   The lexicon form is ἐξέρχομαι (a compound verb made up of εκ and ερχομαι). To figure out what this particular form is, consult the chart of irregular verbs under ἔρχομαι.

4:2   +ὁμολογεῖ   See Bauer and check all the many meanings of this verb to see which one best fits the syntax and context here.

+ἐληλυθότα   This should seem just a little familiar: It is the participle of the perfect tense of ἔρχομαι, which you just looked up in the list of irregular verbs. This is a very irregular and very common verb. It will repay you to memorize its principal parts now, if you have not already done so.

4:3   μὴ ὁμολογεῖ   We expect to see something other than an indicative verb with μή, or, to put it the other way around, we expect to

105

find οὐ as the negative with an indicative verb. Ancient writers, like modern writers, could occasionally have lapses of grammar.

τὸ τοῦ ἀντιχρίστου   A definite article standing by itself (like τό here) usually implies some noun that has been used recently in the text. What is the most recently used neuter singular noun?

ἤδη   an adverb: *already*

4:4   ἐστε   2nd person pl. pres. indic. of εἰμί: *you are*

νενικήκατε   We have met this form previously in 2:13-14. The lexicon form is +νικάω (cf. νίκη, *victory*, the name of a well-known brand of athletic shoes). What are the person, number, tense, and voice of this form?

αὐτούς   Note that this form is masculine, not neuter. What is its antecedent?

4:5   εἰσίν   3rd person pl. pres. indic. of εἰμί: *they are*

λαλοῦσιν   see Bauer s.v. +λαλέω

αὐτῶν ἀκούει   ἀκούω can take its direct object either in the accusative or in the genitive, as here and in the following verse. With an object in the genitive, the verb can mean either *hear* or *listen to*. Cf. Bauer s.v. 1.c.4-5.

4:6   πλάνης   see Bauer and note the relationship to πλανάω

β′ ΓΡΑΜΜΑΤΙΚΑ

The Verb εἰμί (cf. pp. 185-86)

We have encountered forms of the linking verb εἰμί, *be*, with some regularity in our reading — some often enough for them to have become familiar. Like its English equivalent, this verb is quite irregular and has to be learned form by form. It is important enough to merit memorization. The most useful parts to commit to memory are the present and imperfect indicative:

		sg.	pl.
present	1st	εἰμί	ἐσμέν
	2nd	εἶ	ἐστέ
	3rd	ἐστί(ν)	εἰσί(ν)
imperfect	1st	ἤμην	ἦμεν
	2nd	ἦς	ἦτε
	3rd	ἦν	ἦσαν

These forms can also be found on pp. 185-86.

The future indicative (ἔσομαι) uses standard "B" endings and is not irregular. Cf. p. 186.

Contract Verbs (cf. pp. 191-94)

You are used to seeing verbs in the lexicon that end in -άω / -άομαι, -έω / -έομαι, or -όω / -όομαι. Here are ones that you have already encountered: ἀγαπάω, γεννάω, θεωρέω, λαλέω, νικάω, ὁμολογέω, πλανάω, ποιέω, τηρέω, and φανερόω. These are regular O-verbs, but their forms sometimes look a little odd because they undergo contraction. Hence their name: "contract verbs." The vowels with which their stems end (α, ε, or ο) are too weak to remain stable when they are placed side by side with theme vowels. So they merge with the theme vowels in certain regular patterns. Turn to p. 191 for a chart of the ways in which these contractions work.

Some of the final results might be a little difficult to trace back to a lexicon form in -άω, -έω, or -όω. Notice, however, that there is a very useful clue to recognizing forms of these verbs: They usually have a circumflex accent over the theme vowel. We have not attended much to the matter of verb accents, but it is unusual for a verb form to be accented on the ending or theme vowel, unless it is a contract verb. It is important to remember, incidentally, that the uncontracted "lexicon form," which shows the final vowel of the stem, is not an actual form of the verb that could appear in a text of the New Testament: νικάω, for instance, will always be contracted as νικῶ.

Contract verbs live up to their name only in the present and imperfect tenses. In other tenses, the vowel at the end of the verb stem has no opportunity to get entangled with the theme vowel because an infix intervenes between them. But in producing the tenses that use infixes contract verbs do have one small peculiarity: They lengthen the final vowel of the stem: -α and -ε both become -η and -ο becomes -ω. Here are some examples:

	present	future	aorist act.	perfect	aorist pass.
νικάω	νικῶ	νικήσω	ἐνίκησα	νενίκηκα	ἐνικήθην
ποιέω	ποιῶ	ποιήσω	ἐποίησα	πεποίηκα	ἐποιήθην
φανερόω	φανερῶ	φανερώσω	ἐφανέρωσα	πεφανέρωκα	ἐφανερώθην

It is not particularly difficult to get back to the lexicon form from these derived tenses. As long as you get to the right general vicinity in the lexicon, you can usually locate a likely candidate. Then you can check whether you are right by scanning the first paragraph of the entry in the dictionary to see whether forms like the one you are working from are listed as forms of the verb.

In summary, contract verbs are a nuisance mainly in that some of their forms are a little difficult to trace back to the lexicon form. In addition, personal endings or theme vowels sometimes look strange because they have absorbed the last letter of the verb stem. Remember two things:

1. Circumflex accents on the endings or theme vowels of verbs often mean that a contract verb is in use, and
2. if a verb form has an -η- or an -ω- directly before an infix, there is a good chance that it is a contract verb and that the lexicon form will have a different vowel in the same location.

γ´ ΕΞΗΓΗΤΙΚΑ

Using the Lexicon

The Bauer lexicon is full of information — so full that it is somewhat difficult for the beginning student to use. We have chosen it for this course because, unlike "beginner" dictionaries which are quickly exhausted, it will serve as a permanent part of your private exegetical library. The trick in using the Bauer lexicon is to ignore what you do not need to know — and to find what you do need to know.

There are two basic keys: the list of abbreviations and the predictable basic format of the individual entries. Since so much information is packed into the lexicon, much of it, naturally, is abbreviated. Many of the abbreviations are obvious, but many more of them are not. Some of the most important abbreviations for the average user of the lexicon are at the *end* of the list of abbreviations, in section 6 (pp. xxxix-xl of the lexicon). Most of the other abbreviations refer to ancient sources cited as evidence for a certain usage or definition — or to modern discussions of usage. One can hardly sit down and memorize all these abbreviations. The main thing is to know where to find them. The more common ones will become familiar as you use them.

Knowing the basic format of the individual entries will help you find the information that you want when you look a word up. If you are looking a word up for the first time and are only interested in the English translations offered, you may want to skip much of the other information. On the other hand, when you are doing exegesis and trying to dig more deeply into the ancient meaning of a particular text, some of the other bits of information may become more important to you. A typical entry includes the following information:

- full lexicon form (for a noun, this will include gen. sg. and gender; for an adjective, all genders of the nom. sg.; for an irregular verb, the unpredictable forms),
- a brief history of usage (in parentheses),
- English translation(s), in italics, with citations (if the definitions are varied, they will be grouped and numbered),
- "M-M." — an abbreviated reference to another important, but more specialized, lexicon of New Testament Greek, telling you that this word is treated there, and
- * or ** at the end of the entry, meaning that all instances of the word in the literature covered by the Bauer lexicon (*) or just in the New Testament (**) have been cited in the article.

For some illustrations (chosen at random) of how all this works, turn to p. 217 of Bauer. In the middle of the right-hand column you will see an entry for ἐδαφίζω. The first thing it tells you is that it has a slightly irregular future tense: ἐδαφιῶ. (Futures with a circumflex accent like this one are conjugated like -έω contract present tenses.) The usage information tells us that this verb is found in Greek literature from Aristotle onward; in other words, it was a part of Gentile Greek vocabu-

Attic Future

lary. We are also told that it appears in the LXX (= the Septuagint, i.e., the Old Greek Version of the Scriptures of Israel), which means that it might have had some "biblical" associations for the readers of the New Testament. Two English definitions are offered, both of them substantiated with citations from the LXX. Finally, the editors suggest that both meanings are to be found in Luke, where we meet the only New Testament occurrence of the verb.

The next entry, ἔδαφος, is a noun. Therefore its gen. sg. ending is given: The gen. sg. form would be ἐδάφους, which shows that this is a third declension noun like σκότος (see p. 183). The article τό tells you its gender. The usage information shows that the word is an old one, found from Homer onward and also seen in inscriptions and papyri,* suggesting that it was part of the popular, everyday language. It appears commonly in the LXX and various pseudepigrapha. Several references are given, including a major source for papyri (BGU). In earliest Christian literature, it appears only in Acts (Luke again!). A certain pattern appears with regard to Luke's usage — or at least a question: Does Luke particularly like words that would have both a Gentile and a Jewish literary context?

Next we encounter another noun, ἔδεσμα. Its gen. sg. is ἐδέσματος, and τό shows that the gender is neuter. Clearly, this is a third declension noun on the same pattern as ὄνομα (cf. p. 182). We learn that it is used in the earliest Christian literature only in the plural. And the only author included in this lexicon who actually used it was Hermas. Accordingly, it does not appear in the New Testament itself.

The next entry, ἔδομαι, merely refers us to ἐσθίω, since ἔδομαι is an irregular future tense of that verb.

Another verb entry, ἑδράζω, gives us examples of some of its tenses. They are regular, but we will not object to having a little confirmation! This word came into use only in the third century B.C.E., but is found in both Gentile and Jewish authors. From the earliest Christian literature, the entry cites 1 Clement and some letters of Ignatius of Antioch. Since the asterisk tells us the citations are complete, we know there are no New Testament examples.

Finally, at the bottom of the column, we meet ἑδραῖος. The

---

* In this context, the "papyri" in question are not Scripture manuscripts but the whole range of documents dug up from the trash heaps and tombs of Egypt — most of them quite ordinary nonliterary texts such as letters and legal documents.

parentheses around the feminine form of this adjective tell us that the word is sometimes a three-ending adjective and sometimes a two-ending adjective. In the latter case, the "masculine" forms serve as a common gender that includes feminine as well. The word is not cited as having been used by earlier Jewish writers, but it appears a few times in the New Testament and the letters of Ignatius. The entry tells us that it is paired, in Colossians, with τεθεμελιωμένος, which means *founded*.

Obviously, all this information is of varying value depending on what you are looking for. A scholar specializing in New Testament Greek usage or in text criticism may find it very interesting to learn, at the end of the last entry, that ἑδραῖοι is found in one third- to fourth-century papyrus of 1 Pet 5:9 in place of the more usual στερεοί. But most users of the lexicon will probably not care about this. On the other hand, even the relatively casual student may find it useful to observe the mix of Gentile and Jewish usage that prevails here, the way in which words that are rare in the New Testament may have been common in other literature, and the preferences of individual authors for certain vocabulary. All this is in addition to the most basic information about forms, gender, and meaning.

In the next lesson you will begin looking at some vital Johannine vocabulary and at what you can learn about these words from the Bauer lexicon.

LESSON XVII

α' ΛΕΞΙΣ   1 John 4:7-12

4:7 +ἀγαπῶμεν   from +ἀγαπάω (see Bauer)   This form could be a contraction of either ἀγαπάομεν or ἀγαπάωμεν. What is the difference between the two? (The answer is implied in the theme vowel.) How would they be translated differently? Which seems more suitable here?

4:9 ἐν τούτῳ   for this usage of ἐν, see Bauer s.v. III.1, 3.

ἐν ἡμῖν   for this usage of ἐν, see Bauer s.v. I.4.a.

+μονογενῆ   This is a 3rd declension adjective like ἀληθής (see note on 2:8, p. 54). There is some disagreement about the word's meaning, which makes it worthwhile to read the whole entry in Bauer. The definite article before the word serves as "glue" to connect it to the noun it modifies. Given that adjectives must agree with their nouns in gender, number, and case, which noun in the sentence must that be?

+ἀπέσταλκεν   See Bauer s.v. +ἀποστέλλω and pay close attention to the forms in the first paragraph of the entry, since another tense of this verb will appear in the next verse. The form here is perfect active. It lacks a normal reduplication because Greek, on the whole, did not like "s" sounds close together; a number of verb stems that begin with σ- do odd things in the perfect in order to avoid too much sibilance. Do you see the relation of this verb to the noun ἀπόστολος?

112

+ζήσωμεν   see Bauer s.v. +ζάω   What does the combination of -σ- infix and the long theme vowel tell you about tense and mood?

4:10 ἠγαπήκαμεν   The χ-α combination right before the personal ending suggests that this is a perfect tense form. If so, the η might well be a reduplicated α. What is the lexicon form?

ἱλασμὸν   see Bauer   This word is used in the New Testament only here and in 1 John 2:2. In this sentence it is an accusative complement, completing the action of the verb on the direct object, as in the sentence "We elected her president," where "her" is the direct object and "president" is the accusative complement. Greek often, as here, distinguishes the direct object by using the article with it (τὸν υἱὸν αὐτοῦ), leaving the accusative complement "anarthrous" (without an article).

4:11 +οὕτως   *thus*   Adverbs are often made by adding -ως to the basic stem of an adjective. For example, the adverb ἀληθῶς *(truly)* is related to the adjective ἀληθής *(true)*. The demonstrative οὗτος is the source for the adverb οὕτως.

ἀγαπᾶν   present active infinitive of ἀγαπάω: *to love*

4:12 +πώποτε   see Bauer

+τεθέαται   A verb form starting out τεθ- should be looked up under what letter? θ-, the τ being a reduplication. You have seen this verb in 1:1.

+τετελειωμένη ἐστίν   *has been accomplished / completed*
τετελειωμένη is a participle of +τελειόω (see Bauer), but which one? The reduplication and the participial ending are your clues. Our author could perhaps just as well have written a simple perfect passive form, such as τετελείωται, and the meaning would have been no different. But Greek could make a "periphrastic conjugation" in the perfect passive in just the way that you see here — with a participle and the verb εἰμί. It is so very like our English practice that it probably will not give you much trouble.

β΄ ΓΡΑΜΜΑΤΙΚΑ

Infinitives (cf. pp. 186-88)

The infinitive is the only mood of the verb in regular use in Hellenistic Greek that you have not yet studied in any detail.* In English, we have four forms of the infinitive:

	active	passive
present	to make	to be made
perfect	to have made	to have been made

The Greek present infinitives, active and passive, are roughly equivalent in meaning to our present infinitives, and their aorist and perfect infinitives can usually be translated by our perfect infinitives. The only problematic area for us is their future infinitives, which mean something like "to be about to make / be made." Future infinitives are not common in the New Testament.

Here are the forms of the infinitive (cf. pp. 186-88):

	active	middle / passive	middle	passive
present	λύειν	λύεσθαι		
future	λύσειν		λύσεσθαι	λυθήσεσθαι
aorist	λῦσαι		λύσασθαι	λυθῆναι
perfect	λελυκέναι	λελύσθαι		

We are fortunate to be approaching Greek from a background of English, since the two most common uses of the infinitive are essentially the same in the two languages. In your reading of 1 John you have encountered infinitives used for *indirect discourse* and as *verbal complements.* Both uses appeared, for example, in 2:6:

---

* There was one other mood, the optative, inherited from the classical language, but it was used mostly in stereotyped expressions such as μὴ γένοιτο, *may it not happen!* Historically, the optative was used to express a wish or desire.

ὁ λέγων ἐν αὐτῷ μένειν ὀφείλει καθὼς ἐκεῖνος περιεπάτησεν καὶ αὐτὸς περιπατεῖν.

Here, μένειν is the verb in the indirect quotation after λέγων: "the person claiming *to remain* in him." περιπατεῖν complements (i.e., completes the sense of) ὀφείλει: "just as that one walked, he himself ought also *to walk*."

The infinitive is not actually the preferred English way of creating indirect discourse; we prefer a subordinate clause introduced by "that" (cf. Lesson VIII). Still, the infinitive is not completely strange to us in this usage. Perhaps the only point that needs to be added here is that the subject of an infinitive is in the accusative. This is true in English as well as Greek:

* My mother wants *me* to go to the grocery.
* She called ahead and told *them* to reserve a large turkey.
* My sister wasn't doing anything; so I said that I voted for *her* to go instead.

The main difference here between English and Greek is simply that Greek uses the infinitive construction so much more — sometimes in contexts that are a little awkward to translate directly into English.

Complementary use of the infinitive is quite common in English:

* I would like *to go* walking in the rain, but I have *to finish* my work first.
* Life really ought *to be* easier for somebody as deserving as I am.

We have a number of verbs (e.g., "like," "have," and "ought" in these sentences) that require completion by an infinitive in order to have a specific meaning.

Greek, too, has a number of such verbs. A few of the more common are:

ὀφείλω	*ought [to do]*
θέλω	*want, will [to do]*
μέλλω	*be about [to do]*
δεῖ	*must* (lit. *it is necessary [to do]*; always in 3rd person)

Of these, only the first appears in 1 John, but the others are found elsewhere in the New Testament. In particular, δεῖ is a characteristic term in apocalyptic writings, one that expresses the necessity of certain events occurring in accordance with a predetermined divine plan. For example,

> Ἀνάβα ὧδε, καὶ δείξω σοι ἃ δεῖ γενέσθαι μετὰ ταῦτα

Come up here, and I will show you what must happen (lit. *what things it is necessary to happen*) *after these things* (Rev. 4:1).

In short, the complementary use of the infinitive is common in Hellenistic Greek.

A third use of the infinitive, the "articular infinitive," has no analogy in English. It will be discussed in Lesson XXIV.

EXERCISES

Translate the following sentences with examples of

A. Indirect Discourse (use "that" clauses)

1. τὸ πνεῦμα λέγει τὸν θεὸν ἀγαπᾶν (= ἀγαπα-ειν) ὑμᾶς.
2. ἔγραψα ὑμῖν τὸν διάβολον λέγειν ὑμῖν ψεῦδος.
3. λέγετέ μοι ὑμᾶς λαμβάνειν τὴν ἐντολὴν ἡμῶν.

B. Complementary Infinitives

1. τί [Why] μέλλεις ἁμαρτάνειν;
2. οὐκ ὀφείλεις τοῦτο ποιεῖν.
3. θέλω αὐτοὺς τοῦτο μὴ ποιήσειν.
4. δεῖ αὐτοὺς μήποτε τοῦτο ποιῆσαι.

γ′ ΕΞΗΓΗΤΙΚΑ

Some Johannine Vocabulary

In the previous lesson, we saw some examples of the kinds of information a careful reading of Bauer can turn up. Here we apply these skills specifically to a few important items of Johannine vocabulary. One of the interesting things about the vocabulary of the Gospel and the Epistles of John is that it is rather small. Clearly, this is not accidental; the *thought* of the Johannine school, after all, is not particularly simple. For whatever reason, the writers of these documents decided that they could convey their message best by means of a small vocabulary. It is likely, then, that each lexical item is intended to convey something fairly complex and subtle and that we should expect a certain richness of connotation. The lexicon is a helpful place to begin getting a sense of this richness.

As an example, turn to the article on φῶς and look through it briefly. Then read the following commentary on the article.

We already know that the genitive of φῶς is φωτός and that it is a neuter noun of the third declension. The usage information tells us that it is deeply grounded in both Gentile and Jewish literary Greek, besides being found in more popular sources such as inscriptions and papyri. Interestingly, it also made its way into rabbinic literature (in Hebrew or Aramaic) as a loanword, suggesting that it might have been a rather popular religious term.

Like the English *light,* φῶς is likely to have a variety of related meanings and metaphorical uses; but they may not be exactly the same as those of the English word. The lexicon will tell us what scholars have observed about the distinctive use of φῶς in Greek. It is a good idea to begin by checking to see what the overall structure of the article is. The discussion is divided into three parts: Part 1 is clearly labeled "literal," part 3 "the figurative meaning." Part 2 is apparently ambiguous; at least, it is not clearly labeled.

Part 1 is subdivided into a and b, moving, like the article as a whole, from more literal to less literal meanings. 1.a gives us the "general" meaning. One might also say the "most basic" meaning. We are told that φῶς is the opposite of σκότος and that it is not present at night. "Light" in this sense can come from day, from a lamp, or even

from the divine. The latter sense is found in Gentile writers, as we learn
from the citations from Aelius Aristides ("There came a light from Isis")
and from Marinus's *Life of Proclus*, and also in Christian writers. 1.a
also tells us about some "symbolic expressions," i.e., statements talking
about light in the literal sense, but giving it a symbolic reference. The
quotation from Euripides' *Iphigenia among the Taurians* can be translated: "For the night belongs to thieves, but daylight to truth."

1.b gives us meanings that are still literal, but show evidence of
"metonymy," which means "transfer of names," i.e., the transfer of a
noun from one object to a closely related one. We will not be surprised
to find that φῶς can mean "lamp" (though there was also another word
for this: λαμπάς). We make the same shift in English. But we may be a
little more surprised that the term could be applied to fire, the sun,
one's eye, or even (1.b.β) to things illuminated *by* the light.

Section 2 of the article raises the more specific matter of the use
of φῶς in relation to God. It can refer to God as such or, more generally,
to the divine realm. This usage is found in both Gentile and Jewish
authors. In other words, it seems to have belonged to the common
religious parlance of the time. A number of scholarly articles and books
are cited in this section of the article on φῶς, perhaps because this is an
important theological point that has captured a good deal of attention.
You will notice that there are a good many citations from and references
to the Johannine literature, suggesting that this language was particularly important in that literature, though by no means restricted to it,
even among Christian authors. (What other Christian authors are mentioned here?)

The editors of our lexicon do not identify the meanings discussed
in section 2 as "figurative." Many people today would, but the editors
may be right in terms of the mentality of the ancient writers, who might
well have argued that the divine light is the real light and everything
else that we call light is so named only by analogy with the divine.

Finally, in section 3 we come to "figurative meanings," according
to which φῶς is applied to (a) a blessed state of being, (b) bearers of the
gospel, and (c) those who have received the gospel. In this section of
the article, there are still a number of Johannine citations, but there are
many citations of other Christian writers, too. Perhaps these meanings
were relatively less important to the Johannine school — though that is
a question to be determined finally by consulting a concordance.

The article concludes with references to some secondary literature dealing with the use of "light" in the Qumran literature and with its role in the larger context of "Greek optical terminology." Since the understanding of light, its transmission, and its sensory reception was quite different in antiquity from what it is today, such a study would be valuable to anyone who wants to understand this vocabulary thoroughly.

What can you learn by perusing the article on φῶς in this way? This word apparently lent itself readily to being used of the divine sphere. It also had connotations of openness and truthfulness: It was not just a physical or metaphysical term, but also had ethical implications. Since it was a particular favorite of Johannine Christians, we might do well, when we come across it, to ask how its metaphysical and ethical aspects interacted for those Christians.

EXERCISES

With the above discussion of the Bauer article on φῶς as a model, read two articles from the following list and make notes of what interests you and seems important in relation to the Johannine literature. Did Johannine use "specialize," taking only one of several possible meanings as important? Or did it "generalize," using the word in a great variety of senses? What connotations of the word as found in other sources might be important as background for the Johannine use? (Connotations are always a tricky business, and it is wise to be conservative about identifying them. But there is no doubt that they can be important.)

ἀγάπη	ἀδελφός
ἔσχατος	ζωή
κόσμος	παρρησία
σάρξ	ψυχή

LESSON XVIII

α' ΛΕΞΙΣ 1 John 4:13-17

4:13 +δέδωκεν   perfect of δίδωμι

4:14 τεθεάμεθα   thinking about the tense indicators in this verb form will help you locate it in the lexicon

+μαρτυροῦμεν   see Bauer   What English derivatives do you know? How did they derive from the basic meaning of this verb?

ἀπέσταλκεν   if this seems unfamiliar, look back at the previous lesson (4:9)

+σωτῆρα   see Bauer; if the syntax gives you trouble, cf. the note on ἱλασμὸν (4:10, Lesson XVII)

4:15 ὃς ἐὰν   the same as ὃς ἄν; see above, p. 71

4:17 +ἡμέρᾳ   see Bauer

+κρίσεως   see Bauer s.v. κρίσις. This is a 3rd declension noun; see p. 182 for a paradigm. The main peculiarities of this particular kind of 3rd declension noun are the long vowel in gen. sg. and the diphthong in nom. and acc. pl.

β′ ΓΡΑΜΜΑΤΙΚΑ

Verbs with Liquid and Nasal Stems

Liquid consonants are those that can be pronounced (and even pro-
longed) without the aid of a vowel. These include, in Greek, λ and ρ —
and also μ and ν, though they are commonly called "nasals" because of
the other prominent characteristic that they share with each other. When
the stem of an O-verb ends with a liquid or nasal consonant, that creates
a certain problem because these consonants cannot combine, in Greek,
with σ. Since regular future and aorist forms in Greek use a -σ- infix as
a key indicator, this is a bit awkward.

Take, for example, the verb μένω: If it were perfectly regular, we
would expect [μένσω] for future active and [ἔμενσα] for aorist active.
In fact, though, no such forms are found, as we indicate with the brackets
(which are often used in lexica and grammars to indicate unattested
forms presented merely for the sake of completeness or illustration).
Since [μένσω] was impossible, Greek used another distinguishing mark,
an e-vowel that produced the form [μενέω], which in turn was contracted to μενῶ, to distinguish the future tense from the present. This
is, of course, the same kind of contraction that we have encountered in
the present tense of contract verbs. But since μένω is not a contract verb
in the present tense, it can use contract forms to make a distinguishable
future tense, looking like this:

μενῶ	μενοῦμεν
μενεῖς	μενεῖτε
μενεῖ	μενοῦσι(ν)

Contrast these forms with those of the *present tense:*

μένω	μένομεν
μένεις	μένετε
μένει	μένουσι(ν)

Many of the forms are different only in accentuation. Remember that
a circumflex accent on a theme vowel / personal ending frequently in-

dicates that contraction has taken place, and it will help you distinguish present from future tenses in these liquid stem verbs.

There is also a problem with the aorist active and middle, since they, too, normally require a -σ- infix. In this case, the liquid and nasal stem verbs behave a bit more irregularly. Their tendency is to lengthen the stem itself in some way in order to make the aorist a bit different from the present. Thus, in the case of μένω, a "regular" pattern would give the aorist active form [ἔμενσα], but what we actually encounter is ἔμεινα. In the indicative mood this is easy enough to identify as an aorist since it has an augment and an -α- theme vowel. In other moods it is necessary to know the aorist stem as such, for it will be the only thing that distinguishes the aorist subjunctives of these verbs from their present subjunctive forms. μένω, μένῃς, μένῃ, κ.τ.λ., are present subjunctives, as compared with μείνω, μείνῃς, μείνῃ, κ.τ.λ., which are aorist subjunctives.

Some liquid stem verbs are, in effect, irregular verbs (e.g., ἁμαρτάνω, sin). But many follow the general pattern of μένω. We have already encountered ἀποστέλλω, whose future active is ἀποστελῶ (contracted from [ἀποστελέω]) and whose aorist active is ἀπέστειλα.

Other tenses are apt to vary more than the future and the aorist, for example, the perfect forms ἀπέσταλκα and μεμένηκα. The key is simply to remember the characteristic liquid consonants: λ, ρ, μ, and ν. Their presence at the end of a verb stem will signal that you should pay particular attention to what the lexicon entry tells you about the various tense forms.

EXERCISE

Name the tense of each of the following:

μένει	μενεῖ
ἀποστελοῦμεν	ἐμείνατε
μείνωμεν	μενεῖτε
ἀπεστείλαμεν	ἀποστέλλουσι

γ΄ ΕΞΗΓΗΤΙΚΑ

Word Groups

The lexicon tells us not only about individual words, but also about groups of related words. It often happens that if you look forward and backward four or five words in the lexicon from the particular entry you have looked up you will find a number of related words. Not every word in the vicinity is necessarily related: With the noun κρίσις, which you encountered in this lesson's reading, κρίνον, κριός, and the proper name Κρίσπος are not related. On the other hand, κρίμα, κρίνω, κριτήριον, κριτής, and κριτικός are all cognates (relatives) of κρίσις. It can be very helpful to study not a single lexical item at a time, but a group of them.

But first, a word of warning is in order. In any language, the final determinant of meaning is always usage. A word means whatever competent users of the language agree that it means. (To a degree, a word even means whatever I happen to mean by it when I use it, as Humpty Dumpty insisted to Alice. If I want to be understood, however, I should make sure that that meaning is intelligible to others, too.) The relationship of a given word to its near relatives is only one factor among many. Take, for example, this group of English words: justice, judge, judgment, and judgmental. They are related, but they vary from each other in important ways. Justice will certainly not be served if the judge turns out to be judgmental; the judge might even be judged unjust! Yet, taken together, this word group does define a certain range of related meanings. So do the Greek words related to κρίσις, but in their own unique way.

The lexicon gives *judging, judgment* as basic meanings of κρίσις and makes it clear that the word is used heavily in the New Testament and other early Christian literature with reference to the role of God or the Messiah on the Last Day — which is clearly related to its use in this lesson's λέξις. The word tends to have a negative "spin," connoting *condemnation* and *punishment*. Yet, it can also mean "*right* in the sense of *justice, righteousness*." Therefore, its range of meaning is a bit different from that of any one English word.

The verb κρίνω has a similarly broad range of meaning, but is less exclusively tied to formal courtroom procedures. Definitions 1, 2, 3, and

6 emphasize how the verb describes the decisions and judgments of
daily life. It often has a strongly negative sense (see 6.b). At the same
time, definition 4 shows us a strong and well-developed set of usages
related to legal procedure.

The noun κρίμα has a more purely judicial ring to it. This one
might expect just from the form of the word, for nouns formed with
-μα (gen. -ματος) are typically very concrete and refer to specific iden-
tifiable things, while those ending in -σις (like κρίσις) are more apt to
refer to abstract ideas. Notice again the negative quality of the words of
this family. This characteristic is not absolute, but appears to be stronger
than in the equivalent group of English words, where "justice" pulls in
the positive direction. In Hellenistic Greek, in fact, you have to go to
another group of words in order to find a more unambiguously positive
term for "justice," namely δικαιοσύνη. But the associations of δικαιοσύνη are less with courts or administration of justice than with righteousness and vindication.

The remaining words in the group (κριτήριον, κριτής, κριτικός)
are defined primarily in terms of their association with the courts or
the rendering of judgment. The first of them has proven somewhat
difficult to define, particularly in 1 Corinthians 6. The second had, for
those familiar with the Jewish Scriptures, a specific historical reference
to the Israelite "judges" who ruled the people before the time of the
kings. On the whole, these three terms probably add less to our understanding of the word we started with (κρίσις) than do κρίνω and κρίμα.

The result of our study is to confirm for us that κρίσις and related
words are a little different from the English word group containing
justice, judge, and *judgment,* in that they tend to suggest that the judgment will, in fact, be negative — a condemnation. When there was need
to make this unambiguous, Greek could resort to a set of words compounded with the preposition κατά: κατάκριμα, κατακρίνω, κατάκρι-
σις, and κατάκριτος. These refer unambiguously to negative judgment,
condemnation, and punishment. If there was need to refer to the vindication of the accused, however, the whole group of words related to
κρίνω was of less use, and one would usually switch to words related
to δικαιόω instead.

In 1 John 4:17 the expression ἐν τῇ ἡμέρᾳ τῆς κρίσεως is usually
translated "in the day of judgment." If, for the moment, we translated
it "in the day of condemnation," how would that affect the meaning of
the verse? For one thing, it might make it clearer why our author(s)

thinks it is such a great thing to possess παρρησία on that day. Only the person assured of acquittal will have the courage and freedom to speak out boldly on a day dominated by condemnation.

This kind of study can be pursued in more detail in the multi-volume *Theological Dictionary of the New Testament,* familiarly called "Kittel" after its first editor.* This work offers essays on all the major word groups of the New Testament, discussing the history of their use in both Gentile and Jewish literature as well as analyzing their use by early Christian writers. Sometimes the writers in this work were excessively influenced by a particular modern theological stance (that of Barth) and sometimes they forgot the point made at the beginning of this discusion — that, ultimately, all meaning is determined by usage, not by membership of a word in a word group or by etymology. Still, the work is a mine of worthwhile information and many of the individual essays are very fine.

EXERCISE

Study one of the following word groups and determine the range of meanings suggested in Bauer or Kittel. How do the connotations of the word group in Greek differ from those of the usual English translations?

1. ἀγαπάω, ἀγάπη, ἀγαπητός
2. δίκαιος, δικαιοσύνη, δικαιόω, δικαίωμα, δικαίως, δικαίωσις
3. κοινός, κοινωνέω, κοινωνία, κοινωνικός, κοινωνός
4. πιστεύω, πιστικός, πίστις, πιστῶς

---

* See the bibliography in Lesson XXII for details. A one-volume abridgment is also available.

LESSON XIX

α΄ ΛΕΞΙΣ 1 John 4:18-21

4:18 +φόβος   see Bauer   What English derivatives do you know?

+τελεία   see Bauer   What related word(s) do you already know?

+ἔξω   see Bauer

+βάλλει   see Bauer   This is a very common irregular verb, here making its only appearance in the Johannine epistles. See p. 196 for its principal parts.

κόλασιν   see Bauer

+φοβούμενος   This is a participle of φοβέω. See Bauer and notice that this verb appears only in the passive in our literature. The verb's original meaning was *frighten*. In the New Testament it acts like a deponent verb meaning *be afraid*.

4:19 ἀγαπῶμεν   In an α-contract verb it is impossible to be sure whether this form is indicative *we love* (contracted from ἀγαπάομεν) or subjunctive *let us love* (contracted from ἀγαπάωμεν). Which do you think it is — on the basis of context?

+πρῶτος   see Bauer

4:20 +εἴπῃ   see Bauer, s.v. +εἶπον   This verb is commonly used as the aorist of λέγω, but Bauer assigns it its own article. What mood is this form? It seems a little deceptive, since it still appears to have

126

the augment. But it is, in fact, subjunctive, as the ending (with its long vowel) indicates. In this verb, forms with and without augment look the same, e.g., indicative εἶπον, subjunctive εἴπω, infinitive εἰπεῖν, participle εἰπών.

+ἑώρακεν   see Bauer s.v. ὁράω and the chart of irregular verbs, p. 197 below; cf. 1:1

β′ ΓΡΑΜΜΑΤΙΚΑ

Review of Verbs: Tenses

We have already observed that the tenses of the Greek verb do not match up exactly with those of the English verb. We have made use of a simple sort of correlation between the two:

Greek	English	Example
present	present	walk
future	future	will walk
imperfect	continuous past	was walking
aorist	simple past or present perfect	walked / has walked
perfect	present perfect	has walked
pluperfect	past perfect	had walked

This correlation is fine for most purposes, but we are now at a point where we can be a little more exact.

There are three groups of tenses in Greek:

1. the present system (present, future, and imperfect tenses),
2. the perfect system (perfect and pluperfect tenses), and
3. the aorist.

This grouping of tenses makes sense in terms of both the formation of the tenses and their meanings.

The tenses of the *present system* should be thought of primarily as indicating continuous action. For the most part, we translate Greek present tense verbs with the English simple present: λύω means "I untie."

While this is a good rule of thumb, it would be more accurate to think of λύω as fundamentally equivalent to "I am untying." In English, we use the continuous present form only if we wish to emphasize the ongoing quality of the action. That means that we will not always use our continuous present to translate the Greek present tense. But there is always a certain sense of "ongoing-ness" about the Greek present, whether it is made explicit in our translations or not.*

What we have said about the present tense applies also to the future and the imperfect. The future λύσω, in terms of precise meaning, is closer to "I will be untying" than to "I will untie." But we use the simple future to translate the Greek future because our continuous future is used only when we want to emphasize the ongoing quality of the action. Only when translating the imperfect do we consistently use an English continuous form: ἔλυον should be both understood and, for the most part, translated as "I was untying." This is because Greek had two past tenses to our one. It used the aorist in a way equivalent to our simple past ("untied") and reserved the imperfect for those situations where it wanted to stress the ongoing quality of the action.†

The *aorist tense* stands by itself in Greek, not as part of a larger system of tenses. Its name means "unbounded," because, even though it was used chiefly as a past tense, it was not really defined in terms of a particular time. It was defined rather in terms of a particular type of action — the single, punctiliar act. In this respect, it could, given the right circumstances, act as the Greek equivalent of all our simple tenses in English. For example, we tend to state proverbs in the simple present or future: "Watch the pennies and the pounds will take care of themselves"; "Early to bed, early to rise makes one healthy, wealthy, and wise." Classical Greek, on the other hand, tended to put them in the aorist tense; this is called the "gnomic" use of the aorist (from γνώμη, which meant, among other things, "wise opinion").

The aorist tense as we encounter it in the Greek of the New

---

* Compare English verbs that imply, in their definitions, some sort of ongoing action and therefore do not use the continuous present. The verb "have," for example, when used in the sense of "possess," does not form a continuous present; we say, "I have a new car," not "I am having a new car." On the other hand, "have" in the sense of "enjoy," which does not necessarily imply continuity, can be used in the continuous resent: "I am having dinner now."

† This is why a verb whose meaning indicates a state of being rather than a simple action may not even have an aorist; εἰμί, *to be*, has only present, future, and imperfect tenses.

Testament has somewhat different functions depending on the mood in which it is being used. In the indicative, it refers almost exclusively to single actions performed in the past. The one problem we encounter here is with English — which has not one, but two ways of indicating single past actions. If someone says "It's raining. Are the windows open?" you can reply "I closed them" or "I have closed them" with no practical difference between the two responses. Accordingly, the Greek aorist ἔλυσα can be translated "I untied" or "I have untied" — whichever seems to suit the flow of the English translation better.

In moods other than the indicative, the aorist has very little sense of time at all. It retains some in the participle, which we will discuss in Lesson XXI. In the subjunctive and infinitive, however, if the aorist is at all different from the present tense, it is purely a matter of single, punctiliar action (aorist) as distinguished from linear or continuous action (present). This is most obvious in the imperative, where the present tense tends to have the implication "Go on untying" (λῦε) or "Stop untying" (μὴ λῦε), while the aorist would imply a specific act: "Untie it" (λῦσον) or "Don't untie it" (μὴ λῦσον). These distinctions are not absolute, since language is never totally law-abiding, but they are at least a good guide to the nuances involved.

If the aorist is a bit strange to our thinking, the *perfect system* is probably more so. We can get by, pretty easily, translating Greek perfects as English present perfects (λέλυκα = "I have untied") and Greek pluperfects as English past perfects (ἐλελύκειν = "I had untied"). That may leave us wondering, however, why Greek had two tenses (aorist and perfect) that were the equivalent of our present perfect. It might also, eventually, make us wonder why the perfect tense, in Greek, is much less common than our present perfect.

The Greek perfect tense conveyed something for which we do not have a straightforward tense form in English: It refers to past action that determines a present situation. There are certain informal English idioms using the verb "get" that convey this information, but they do not seem to have a name in our grammar. Compare the following examples:

- "Are the windows closed?" "Yes, I got them closed."
- "I got the water out of the basement, too."
- "Did we get water in the basement?!"
- "If it had gotten any deeper, your library would have been soaked."

In the first line, the reply indicates that the windows are still closed as the result of a past action. The second implies that the basement is now reasonably dry, as the result of a past action. The third asks a question about an event that produced an ongoing state. And in the last line, "had gotten any deeper" is the equivalent of a Greek pluperfect, indicating a past event determining a *past* state (both of which have not actually happened). The verbs with "get" in the first three lines are equivalents of Greek perfects, indicating past events that determine the *present* state at the time of speaking.

It is rarely necessary, in translating the Greek perfect tense, to make all this fully explicit. After all, the English perfect tenses *can* be the equivalent of the Greek perfect system. For example:

- "I have finished my degree program and have gotten the job I wanted."
- "My friend and I have started our vacation."
- "I had just dressed for dinner when the earthquake hit."

In the first of these examples, the implication is that the speaker still has both the degree and the job. In the second, the implication is that speaker and friend are both still on vacation. And the third implies that the speaker was garbed for the meal when the ground started shaking.

But an English perfect may be used to represent something less complex in the Greek text, that is, a plain aorist. It would be a mistake to pin too much on a perfect tense in the English translation. The exegete needs to know what Greek tense lies behind it.

EXERCISE

What Greek tense(s) would be most nearly equivalent to the italicized English words?

1. What *were you doing* before you *came* to dinner?
2. I *was reading* a novel.
3. As you can see, I *have mopped* the floor.
4. *Are you suggesting* that I *was being* lazy?
5. What *made* you think that?

6. The way you *looked* at me.
7. You *were reading* too much into that.
8. I've *worked* hard today and it *has tired* me out.

γ΄ ΕΞΗΓΗΤΙΚΑ

Using a Concordance (I)

One of the best tools for studying Scripture is a concordance. You may use a concordance, of course, as a kind of index, allowing you to look up a passage that you remember but cannot remember where to find. That in itself is useful. But the concordance also helps with exegesis. It allows us to get a quick overview of the use of a particular word in Scripture and to answer a whole series of questions that would otherwise be hard to answer — such as:

- Is this a common word?
- Who else among the biblical writers used it?
- Is it a favorite word of some particular group of biblical writers?
- Does the particular author I am reading use it much?
- Does this author use it in an unusual way?
- What does this author, in particular, seem to mean by it?
- With what other words or ideas does this author associate use of this word?

By bringing together passages using the same word, a good concordance makes it relatively easy to ask these and similar questions.

Of course, to do this sort of study, you need access to the Greek vocabulary of a New Testament writing, not just its English translation. Translations can be misleading, since the same Greek word may be translated in several different ways and a single English word may represent several different Greek words. The most efficient way to find out how an author is using Greek vocabulary is to check in a concordance of the Greek New Testament, such as the one originally edited by W. F. Moulton and A. S. Geden and revised several times in this century. This can be frustrating, however, for the new student of Greek, who will not yet be able to understand all of the citations. On the other hand, most

English concordances cover only a particular English translation and give no insight into the Greek text behind it.

Fortunately, there are also "analytical" concordances available, such as *Young's Analytical Concordance* and *Strong's Exhaustive Concordance*, both based on the King James Version, and a more recent one, *The Eerdmans Analytical Concordance to the Revised Standard Version of the Bible.** Of these, the latter is much better since it refers to a more modern translation and a more reliable text of the Greek New Testament lies behind it.

Using one or the other of these analytical concordances, it is relatively easy to investigate some of the interesting features of Johannine vocabulary. For example, we have encountered the noun παρρησία in 1 John. Begin by looking it up in the list of Greek words at the back of the concordance; there you will find the English translations used in either the KJV or RSV. You can then turn, in the main part of the concordance, to the English words noted and find whether this is a word unique to the Johannine literature or whether it is widespread in the New Testament writings. See whether the other instances, if any, shed light on what the author(s) of 1 John mean by it, or whether the usage in 1 John is highly distinctive. Use the questions suggested above in your study.

Do the same with two other words: πλανάω (check πλάνη, too) and φοβέομαι (also φόβος).

The lexicon is our first recourse for understanding the meanings of words, but the question of how a particular author is using a term can often best be resolved by thinking through the data made available in a concordance. When you are trying to interpret a particular passage, it is often worthwhile to select some key words from it to look up in the concordance.

---

* See the bibliography in Lesson XXII.

LESSON XX

α' ΛΕΞΙΣ 1 John 5:1-5

5:1 τὸν γεννήσαντα . . . τὸν γεγεννημένον These two participles give a good illustration of the difference between the aorist and perfect tenses: Both refer to a past action, but the perfect participle refers specifically to a past action that has determined a present situation. The aorist active participle here *(the one having begotten)* seems to treat God's begetting as a simple past act; but in reference to the Son, the *perfect passive* participle is more appropriate, since the Son remains *the one begotten* long after the act of begetting is past.

ἀγαπᾷ contracted from [ἀγαπάει]

5:3 αὕτη note the accent and breathing mark

βαρεῖαι see Bauer s.v. βαρύς and be sure to notice the full range of figurative meanings

5:4 πᾶν τὸ γεγεννημένον What is the gender? Why?

νικᾷ contracted from [νικάει]

+νίκη see Bauer, but you can probably guess!

νικήσασα The feminine participle is less common than masc. or neut. What are the tense and voice here?

+πίστις see Bauer This is a very important New Testament

133

noun, but it is very rare in the Johannine literature, which prefers
the related verb πιστεύω.

τίς   notice the accent and the punctuation of the sentence

β' ΓΡΑΜΜΑΤΙΚΑ

Review of Verbs: Forms

This is a good point in our progress to consolidate what we know
about verb forms and put the information into a somewhat more
orderly state. We have learned many individual pieces of information,
but the larger picture may still seem obscure. In learning grammar, it
is necessary to keep moving back and forth between the larger picture
and the details.

There are three ways to organize your knowledge of verb forms
and it is best to use all three:

1. One way is to consider what kinds of information the verb conveys
   and to organize your knowledge accordingly. These kinds of information are: person, number, tense, voice, mood, and, in participles, gender and case. These kinds of information are embodied
   in verb forms in several ways:

   • *Person* — 1st, 2nd, or 3rd — is expressed by the personal ending
     of the verb.
   • *Number* — singular or plural — is also expressed by the personal
     endings, except in participles, which act like adjectives in this
     regard and express number in case endings.
   • *Tense* — present, imperfect, future, aorist, perfect, or pluperfect —
     is expressed by a combination of alterations at the beginning of
     the verb stem (augments, reduplications), infixes between the verb
     stem and the personal ending (-σ-, -κ-, -θ-, -θησ-), and theme
     vowels "gluing" the personal ending to the verb stem or to the
     infix.
   • *Voice* — active, middle, or passive — is expressed by various com-
     binations of infixes and personal endings ("A" endings are active

except in the aorist passive subjunctive; "B" endings are middle or passive but with active *meaning* in deponent verbs).

- *Mood* — indicative, subjunctive, imperative, infinitive, or participle — is expressed by augment (indicative of past tenses), by the length and type of theme vowel, and by specific endings (as in some forms of the imperative and all the infinitive and participle endings).

2. You can organize the same information in a manner closer to the way you have been learning it by thinking about the forms themselves and how the forms convey the information they convey. Every verb form includes some or all of the following informational "slots":

- A *prefix* (e.g., ἀποστέλλω, ἐξέρχομαι, ἀφίημι) must be mentally subtracted in order to analyze the basic verb form.
- *Augment* (e.g., ἔλυσα, ἠγάπησε, περιεπάτησεν) takes the form of an ε or of a lengthening of the initial vowel of the stem and tells us that we are dealing with the indicative mood of a past tense (imperfect, aorist, or pluperfect).
- *Reduplication* (e.g., λέλυκα, τεθέαμαι, ἠγάπηκα) doubles the initial consonant (adjusting for the aspirated consonants θ, φ, and χ) with the help of -ε- or lengthens the initial vowel and tells us that we are dealing with the perfect system (perfect or pluperfect tenses).*
- The *verb stem* (e.g., ἐλελύκειν, ἀποστέλλομεν, λύω, ἔρχομαι) conveys the lexical meaning of the particular verb and in irregular verbs (including those with 2nd aorists) suffers some alteration to indicate the various tenses.
- The *infix* (e.g., λύσω, ἠγάπησα, πεποίηκεν, ἐφανερώθη, λυθήσομαι), -σ-, -κ-, -θ-, or -θησ-, in combination with other elements such as augments or reduplications, tells us about the verb's tense or voice (or both).
- The *theme vowel* comes in six basic types:

  e / o in the present system and in 2nd aorist (e.g., λύεις, λύομεν),

---

* There are also, of course, reduplications with -ι- in the present and imperfect tenses of some MI-verbs (such as δίδωμι, τίθημι, and ἵστημι).

α in 1st aorist and perfect active (e.g., ἐλύσᾱτε, λελύκαμεν),

η in aorist passive (e.g., ἐλύθητε),

ει in pluperfect active (e.g., ἐλελύκειν, ἐλελύκειμεν),

long e / o in subjunctives (e.g., λύωμεν, λύησθε), or

no theme vowel in perfect and pluperfect passive.

The theme vowel tells us, in combination with augments, reduplications, and infixes, about tense and mood.

- The verb's *ending* comes in three basic types ("A" or active, "B" or middle-passive, and the somewhat distinct endings of the aorist passive) and tells us about voice, person, and number (in indicative, imperative, and subjunctive) and often tense and mood as well.

3. A third way of organizing the material is by **identifying characteristics of tense formation.**

Present System

Present tense: basic stem + e / o theme vowels

Imperfect tense: augment + basic stem + e / o theme vowels + distinctive endings

Future active or middle: basic stem + -σ- infix + e / o theme vowels

Future passive: basic stem + -θησ- infix + e / o theme vowels

Aorists

1st Aorist active or middle: augment (indicative only) + basic stem + -σ- infix + α theme vowel

2nd Aorist active or middle: augment (indicative only) + altered stem + e / o theme vowel

Aorist passive: augment (indicative only) + basic stem + -θ- infix* + η theme vowel

---

* The infix is missing in some aorist passives, often called "second aorist passives."

Perfect System

> Perfect active: reduplication + basic stem + -ϰ- infix + α theme vowel
>
> Perfect middle-passive: reduplication + basic stem + *no* theme vowel
>
> Pluperfect active: augment* + reduplication + basic stem + -ϰ- infix + ει theme vowel
>
> Pluperfect passive: usually formed "periphrastically" (perfect passive participle with past tense of εἰμί)

With these three approaches to organization in mind, review the verb forms in the paradigms on pp. 186-90. They will help you get from the word in the text to some sense of its meaning. It will also be worth your effort to memorize the paradigms that include some of the more common forms, especially now that you already know many of the forms. The following would be a good list:

- present indicative
- present subjunctive
- present imperative
- present participles
- present infinitives
- imperfect indicative
- aorist active indicative
- aorist active and middle imperatives
- aorist active and middle infinitives
- aorist passive indicative
- aorist passive imperative
- aorist passive infinitive
- perfect indicative
- perfect infinitive

Other forms can be identified by comparison with these. For example, future tense forms are practically identical to present tense forms, with just the infixes showing the difference. Aorist subjunctives differ from present forms only by their infixes. Aorist middles differ from aorist actives only by using "B" endings. Pluperfects are fairly rare and usually easy to recognize.

* Often lost in Hellenistic Greek.

EXERCISE

To "parse" a verb is to give all of the following information that is applicable to a particular form: person, number, tense, voice, mood, gender, number, case, and lexicon form. Parse the following forms of λύω, γράφω, and φανερόω on the basis of the rules given above, looking at the paradigms as little as possible.

λέλυκας	ἐλύθησαν
ἔγραψα	λύσουσι
γράφοντες	λύσωμεν
λυόμεθα	γράφειν
λύωμεν	φανερουμένη
πεφανέρωκε	ἔγραφες
λυθέντος	γράψεις
ἐλελύκειμεν	φανερώσεσθε
φανερωθησόμεθα	

γ΄ ΕΞΗΓΗΤΙΚΑ

Using a Concordance (II)

The concordance helps you learn not only about the meaning of a particular word in the language of the first century but also about how a specific author uses language. For example, the author(s) of 1 John like to use kinship language of relationships in the Christian community. For example, they often address the readers as "little children" (παιδία, τεκνία).*

Going on from this observation, it will be useful to look at the use of other kinship terms in the letter with the help of the concordance. For instance, is τέκνον used in the same way as the diminutive τεκνίον? What about other words for children, such as "son" (υἱός) or "daughter" (θυγάτηρ)? Are they used and, if so, how? Why? Where do words for parents (πατήρ, μήτηρ) appear? To whom are they applied? Do the

---

* Perhaps we should translate these terms simply as "children." Although both words are diminutives in form, it is hard to be sure how different in meaning diminutives were from their original forms in Hellenistic Greek.

author(s) regard themselves as "parents"? To whom are words for sib-lings (ἀδελφός, ἀδελφή) applied? Why are our authors so interested in these terms?

Since every writer has a somewhat individualized way of using language, the concordance offers valuable insight into what linguists sometimes call the writer's "idiolect." Most of us call this "style," but we need to remember that style and substance are not opposites — at least not in writings of enduring value. Ideally, style and substance are two aspects of the same thing. The significance of 1 John is found in the way that the author approaches the audience as well as in specific information and directives passed along. A concordance is a valuable tool for getting at the connection between substance and expression in any literary work.

LESSON XXI

5:6   +ἐλθών   2nd aorist active participle of ἔρχομαι   2nd   aorist
active participles look like present active participles except that
they are accented on a different syllable.

+ὕδατος, ὕδατι   the nominative form is ὕδωρ

+αἵματος, αἵματι   the nominative form is αἷμα   Do you recognize any English derivatives?

μαρτυροῦν   contracted from [μαρτυρέον], neut. nom. sg. present act. participle of μαρτυρέω

5:7   +τρεῖς   *Three,* declined as follows:

	m. / f.		n.
nom.	τρεῖς		τρία
gen.		τριῶν	
dat.		τρισίν	
acc.	τρεῖς		τρία

5:8   +οὐρανῷ in the textual apparatus   οὐρανός, *heaven*   Be sure
to note the long variant reading in n. 4 to v. 8. It is often referred
to as the Johannine "comma" (i.e., "clause"). Exclusion of it from
the text of 1 John on text-critical grounds has sometimes stirred
up anger because it is the closest the New Testament comes to an
explicit statement of the later doctrine of the Trinity. You can see
from the apparatus that it has very little support in Greek — and

140

that only in very late mss. Support for it goes back farther in the Latin-speaking West.

ἕν   Note the breathing mark and accent. If still perplexed, look at Lesson XIII, p. 85, the note on 3:7.

5:9   +μαρτυρίαν   see Bauer

+ἀνθρώπων   see Bauer   Note that this is the word for "human being," though it can sometimes refer specifically to an adult male human being. But Greek did have a separate word for "adult male human being": ἀνήρ, gen. ἀνδρός.

5:1   +ἔδωκεν   the somewhat irregular aorist active indicative of δίδωμι

αὕτη ἡ ζωή   This is the usual way of saying *this life* in Greek: The article is acting as "glue" to connect the noun and the demonstrative and cannot be represented in the English translation.

β′ ΓΡΑΜΜΑΤΙΚΑ

Tenses in Participles

The tenses of Greek participles work a bit differently from tenses in the other moods. Happily, though, they work just as they do in English participles, so that our problem is not to learn something new, but to remind ourselves of something we already know and to apply it to Greek. The main point to remember is that the tenses of participles are always *relative*. Participles cannot, for the most part, function as main verbs.* That means that they are always in some subordinate role. The main verb of the sentence determines the time frame of the sentence as a whole; any participles in the sentence indicate nothing more than time in relation to the main verb.

Here are some examples in English:

1. Having gotten into the car, we set off for St. Dorothy's Rest.

---

* Occasionally a participle could substitute for an imperative in Greek.

2. Driving along the highway, we encountered a lot of crazy motorists.
3. Passing through the Sebastopol area, we admired the apple orchards.
4. Having left the town, we ran out of gas.
5. Getting back and forth from a gas station, we lost an hour.
6. Being eager to see the redwoods, we found it was already dark when we arrived.

All the main verbs in these sentences ("set," "encountered," "admired," "ran," "lost," "found") are past tense. Some of the participles are *present participles,* namely "driving," "passing," "getting," and "being." Present participles indicate not that these events took place in the speaker's present (i.e., as the narrator was actually speaking), but rather that they took place *at the same time as the action of the main verb.* The other participles here ("having gotten" and "having left") are *perfect participles;* they indicate events that took place *before the action of the main verb.*

We could easily convert all the participial phrases above into dependent clauses. For the present participles, we would use conjunctions like "while" and "as." For the perfect participles, we would use "after."

1. After we got into the car, we set off for St. Dorothy's Rest.
2. As we drove along the highway, we encountered a lot of crazy motorists.
3. As we passed through the Sebastopol area, we admired the apple orchards.
4. After we left the town, we ran out of gas.
5. While we were getting back and forth from a gas station, we lost an hour.
6. While we were eager to see the redwoods, we found it was already dark when we arrived.

There are several other possible ways of presenting the ideas in these sentences in English. The point here is simply that the perfect participles always represent time before that of the main verb, while the present participle represents time the same as that of the main verb.

Another way of illustrating this is to change the time of the main verbs in these sentences:

1. Having gotten into the car, we *will* set off for St. Dorothy's Rest.
2. Driving along the highway, we *will* no doubt encounter a lot of crazy motorists.
3. Passing through the Sebastopol area, we *will* be able to admire the apple orchards.
4. Having left the town, we *may* run out of gas.
5. Getting back and forth from a gas station, we *will* lose an hour.
6. Being eager to see the redwoods, we *will* find it is already dark when we arrive.

Such foreboding, of course, might keep you from taking the trip. But in a more purely grammatical vein, notice that the participles do not have to change at all to accommodate the change of tenses in the main verbs. Present participles still indicate time the same as that of the main verb, perfect participles time before that of the main verb.

Greek works by the same rules. Present participles indicate time the same as that of the main verb, whatever tense that verb may be. Aorist and perfect participles indicate time before that of the main verb, whatever tense that verb may be, and differ from each other only in that aorist participles usually indicate simple, punctiliar actions while perfect participles indicate actions that have determined a subsequent state of affairs.

Greek also had a set of future participles to indicate events expected to follow the time of the main verb. We have no convenient English equivalent, but we can approximate such a participle in this way: "*Being about to reach* the crest of the ridge, we sat down first to catch our breath." The equivalent subordinate clause might read: "Just before we reached the crest of the ridge, we sat down to catch our breath."

EXERCISE

Rewrite the following sentences, turning their participial phrases into dependent clauses with "while," "as," or "after."

1. Floating in a tube on the river, I was carried slowly downstream.
2. Having bobbed along for a while, I ran aground in the shallows.
3. Being under some trees, I decided to stop there a while.

4. Having gotten out of the tube, I lay on the sandbar.
5. The wind rising, the day got colder.
6. Looking for my tube, I found it gone.
7. Gazing downstream, I saw it caught on a tree root.
8. Having swum over to it, I retrieved it and started home.

γ΄ ΕΞΗΓΗΤΙΚΑ

The Importance of Context

Much of the knowledge that an exegete needs may be thought of as
knowledge of *context* — or, better, *contexts*. In order to read and interpret a document written many centuries ago in a world quite different
from our own, we need to learn what we can about the historical context
of the document and, what is perhaps even more important, about its
cultural context, including the language in which it was written. Language is a cultural artifact; to understand a language requires understanding of the culture to which it gave expression.

Even knowledge that at first sight seems remote from a text may
turn out to be important for understanding it. Christian readers are
likely to be applying their historical knowledge of the origins of Chris-
tianity to their reading of 1 John even when they are quite unconscious
of doing so. Knowledge of ancient Mediterranean family patterns will
help the reader catch nuances in the author's habit of addressing the
audience as τεχνία or describing them as ἀδελφοί. Now that you are
learning Greek, a perfect tense such as νενιχήχατε may well have more
meaning for you than before, since it means not only "you have con-
quered" in the sense of a completed past act (the usual meaning of the
present perfect in English), but also "your conquest still holds good."
Thus, every kind of general knowledge that you can gain about the
language and world in which the New Testament authors wrote is likely
to increase your appreciation of some aspect of their meaning.

Within the New Testament itself, we have seen how investigating
vocabulary with the help of the lexicon and the concordance can show
us interesting and helpful things about how the early Christians used
the language they shared with others, both Jewish and Gentile. Some
words, such as χριστός or χύριος, were used in roughly the same way

by a great variety of Christian authors. But a particular writer or group of writers might attach special meanings or special importance to certain other words or phrases, such as ζωή or φῶς in the Johannine literature. This, too, is a matter of context, though now it is context of a narrower sort — no longer the larger cultural and historical context of the ancient Mediterranean world, but the more specific (one might say "subcultural") context peculiar to the Christian communities.

Finally, one must also consider, for any given text, the quite specific context of the text's immediate literary location. This may mean something as broad as the whole book in which it is found or something as narrow as the paragraphs directly preceding and following it. How many people have read, enjoyed, referred to, been inspired by, even preached from the great encomium on love in 1 Corinthians 13 without ever noticing that it is part of a larger argument that Paul is constructing, in chapters 12–14, against those who were making excessive claims on behalf of the gift of speaking in tongues? But noticing this actually enhances the power and significance of the passage: It is not simply a bit of inspired rhetoric divorced from real-life concerns; it is, rather, Paul's response to a situation where the piety of individuals was threatening the coherence of the whole church community. It is about real human and Christian life. To discover that in this particular case, one needs only read one chapter before and one after the text itself.

To get at the immediate literary context of a passage, one reads the materials before and after and asks how they are all connected together. It is also important to see how the passage fits into the book as a whole. One useful approach to this is to outline the book. This may be most practicable when you know that you will be dealing with a particular book over a period of time, as when you are preparing a series of sermons or getting ready to teach a course. But when you do not have the time or occasion to do the task for yourself, you will find that most commentaries will offer you some sort of outline of the book. Often, it is instructive to compare a variety of outlines, your own and those of others.

Yet another way into the literary context is through the concordance. In 1 John, the terms μαρτυρέω and μαρτυρία are found almost exclusively in the reading in this lesson. Given the amount of repetition in the vocabulary of this little work, that is surprising in and of itself. Perhaps even more interesting is the fact that the only instances of these

words elsewhere in the book are where the author(s) are emphasizing
their own reliability:

καὶ ἑωράκαμεν καὶ μαρτυροῦμεν καὶ ἀπαγγέλλομεν ὑμῖν τὴν
ζωὴν τὴν αἰώνιον (1:2)

καὶ ἡμεῖς τεθεάμεθα καὶ μαρτυροῦμεν ὅτι ὁ πατὴρ ἀπέσταλκεν
τὸν υἱὸν σωτῆρα τοῦ κόσμου (4:14)

Notice, too, that witnessing is strongly associated with vision here: One
can only witness to what one has seen. Does this association lie behind
the usage in 5:6-12, too? What validates witness in this passage? How is
witness related to the tradition that the author(s) emphasized so
strongly in the opening of the book? Questions like these are a way of
discovering the interrelationship of a particular text to the larger whole
of which it is a part. Outlining and the use of the concordance are two
of the best ways of raising such questions and seeking answers to them.

LESSON XXII

5:13 +εἰδῆτε   2nd person pl. perf. act. subj. of οἶδα   You have learned this verb's perfect indicative (which has the meaning of a present tense) in Lesson XIII (p. 84 above). The perfect subjunctive is:

	sg.	pl.
1	εἰδῶ	εἰδῶμεν
2	εἰδῇς	εἰδῆτε
3	εἰδῇ	εἰδῶσι

The infinitive is εἰδέναι. The pluperfect, which acts as the all-purpose past tense of this verb, is ᾔδειν, ᾔδεις, κ.τ.λ. (η being an augmented form of ει). Occasionally, you will see a future tense, in the form of either εἰδήσω or εἴσομαι.

Clearly, the basic stem of this verb is not οἰδ- but εἰδ-. It is related to Latin *video*, "see." The perfect tense "I have seen" slowly shifted to meaning "I know." The main problems that arise are (1) recognizing that a number of forms beginning with εἰδ- / ᾐδ- are really related to οἶδα and (2) distinguishing these from other forms of this same root that form the aorist tense (εἶδον) of ὁράω, *see*. On this last point, see the note below on 5:16.

τοῖς πιστεύουσιν πιστεύουσιν could conceivably be the 3rd person pl. present act. indicative of πιστεύω: *they believe*. The presence of the definite article τοῖς, however, signals that it is in

147

fact the dative plural masc. or neut. present active participle: *to the ones believing.* The two forms are identical and have to be distinguished on a case by case basis. The participle is dative plural here because it modifies an earlier dative plural in the sentence. There is only one candidate — which word is it?

5:14 +αἰτώμεθα   see Bauer, s.v. αἰτέω   There is no distinction of meaning between the active and middle voices in this verb. Since we will be seeing several different forms of this verb in the next few verses, it may be worthwhile to think about what they should look like. The verb begins with a diphthong, αι-, which is lengthened to η- when it is augmented or reduplicated. It is also an ε-contract verb, which means that the last letter of the stem will either be contracted with the theme vowel or else be lengthened to -η- before an infix. A few forms, by way of example: imperfect active indicative is ᾐτοῦν, future active indicative is αἰτήσω, aorist active indicative is ᾔτησα, and perfect active indicative is ᾔτηκα.

+κατὰ τὸ +θέλημα   see Bauer   A good way to remember the significance of κατά with accusative is to memorize the names of the Gospels in Greek: Κατὰ Μαθθαῖον, Κατὰ Μᾶρκον, κ.τ.λ.

ἀκούει ἡμῶν   Remember that ἀκούω can take its direct object in either the accusative or the genitive case. This becomes important in the following verse as well.

5:15 ὃ ἐὰν αἰτώμεθα   for the relative pronoun plus ἐάν or ἄν, see above, p. 71   Here, the whole relative clause serves as a direct object of ἀκούει, which has, however, *two* direct objects here, the other being ἡμῶν. This is a little awkward to translate into English.

τὰ +αἰτήματα   see Bauer   Greek nouns formed with the ending -μα (gen. -ματος) express an element of "thingness." Thus, for example, αἴτημα is *what you ask for / request,* πνεῦμα is *what you breathe,* i.e., *breath, wind, spirit,* and θέλημα is *what you want / will* (from the verb θέλω, *will, want*).

ᾐτήκαμεν   if this form is puzzling, see the note on αἰτώμεθα in v. 14

5:16 +ἴδῃ   3rd person sg. aor. act. subj. of εἶδον, the irregular 2nd aorist of ὁράω.   The subjunctive forms are ἴδω, ἴδῃς, ἴδῃ, κ.τ.λ. The infinitive is ἰδεῖν. The participle is ἰδών, ἰδοῦσα, ἰδόν. Cf. the forms of the related verb οἶδα in the notes on v. 13.

ἁμαρτάνοντα ἁμαρτίαν   *sinning a sin* This so-called *figura etymologica* (etymological device) is a rhetorical figure more at home in Hebrew than in either Greek or English, where *sinning* would be enough. Why is the present participle used here? What exactly does it convey?

δώσει   future of δίδωμι

τοῖς ἁμαρτάνουσιν   another dative plural participle; cf. above on v. 13

μή   This negative is used because it is in a participial phrase; contrast οὐ πρὸς θάνατον at the end of v. 17, where the verb (ἔστιν) is indicative.

ἔστιν   Placing the linking verb at the beginning of the clause, as here, emphasizes it: "There *is*. . . ."

+ἐρωτήσῃ   see Bauer s.v. ἐρωτάω

β΄ ΓΡΑΜΜΑΤΙΚΑ

Participles and Subordinate Clauses

We have already seen above (Lesson XII) that Greek participles, when used with the definite article, were often equivalent to English relative clauses. In this lesson, we will be looking at another type of subordinate clause in English and seeing how it, too, can be equivalent to a kind of participial clause in Greek.

First, though, a word about clauses. Every sentence must have a *main clause,* including a subject, a verb,* and whatever complements the verb may require, such as direct object, predicate nominative,

* Greek can omit the actual verb if it is clearly implied. It often omits linking verbs.

adverbs, or prepositional phrases. Many sentences, called *simple sentences,* consist of nothing more than a main clause:

1. The sun was warm.
2. The breeze was chilly.
3. We were following the trail.
4. We found ourselves on an exposed hillside.
5. We looked for a snug spot, out of the wind.
6. We had brought no jackets.

Each such sentence contains only one main clause and no subordinate clauses.

A slightly more complicated way of speaking (though we scarcely feel it as such) is to string such simple sentences together with "coordinating conjunctions" such as *and, or, but,* and *for* (καί, ἤ, δέ, ἀλλά, and γάρ). Each clause is still an independent statement, but the connections between them are more explicit:

1. The sun was warm, but the breeze was chilly.
2. We were following the trail and we found ourselves on an exposed hillside.
3. We looked for a snug spot, out of the wind, for we had brought no jackets.

These are called *compound sentences* because they combine (or "compound") two or more main clauses into a single sentence.

Finally, a more nuanced way of putting clauses together is to choose some to serve as main clauses and make the rest of the clauses subordinate to the main clauses. To do this, in English, we use either relative pronouns or "subordinating conjunctions" such as *since, as, if, when, where, although,* etc. The result is a set of *complex sentences:*

1. Although the sun was warm, the breeze was chilly.
2. We who were following the trail found ourselves on an exposed hillside.
3. We looked for a snug spot, out of the wind, since we had brought no jackets.

The *subordinate clauses* here are the clauses that begin with either a relative pronoun or a subordinating conjunction.

Greek, like English, uses both relative pronouns and subordinating conjunctions. We have met the relative pronoun (and its variants ὅστις and ὃς ἐάν) and a few subordinating conjunctions (ἐάν, ἵνα, ὅτι). But Greek was also inclined to use participles much more freely than English to do the same work. Sometimes it is important to be able to tell just what task a given participle is doing. It is a good rule of thumb that when Hellenistic Greek wanted a participle to do the work of a relative pronoun it put an article before it, and when it wanted the participle to do the work of a subordinating conjunction it did not use an article.

Good

Almost all the participial clauses we have seen in 1 John have had the article. You have learned that it is suitable to substitute a relative clause in translating these participles. Now, in this lesson's reading, you have an example of a participle without an article:

'Εάν τις ἴδη τὸν ἀδελφὸν αὐτοῦ ἁμαρτάνοντα ἁμαρτίαν μὴ πρὸς θάνατον, αἰτήσει, καὶ δώσει αὐτῷ ζωήν. . . . (5:16)

Here it would be best *not* to use a relative clause in your translation, since the absence of the article in the Greek suggests that the nuance is a bit different. The point is not "If anyone sees his brother *who* is sinning . . . ," but rather "If anyone sees his brother *as* he is sinning. . . ."

Subordinate clauses that begin with relative pronouns are called *substantive clauses* because they can function as adjectives or in any of the roles that nouns take in a sentence:

subject	*Whoever gets there first* should set up camp.
direct object	Use *whatever wood you find* to start the fire.
modifier	The one *who has the truck* will bring the groceries.

Subordinate clauses that begin with subordinating conjunctions are called *adverbial clauses*. They provide the answers to questions such as "When?" "Where?" "How?" and "Under what circumstances?" For example:

If you get there first, set up camp.
Since we have no campstove, gather wood and build a fire.
When the truck gets there, we will have groceries.

English can use participles as substitutes for some adverbial

clauses. Two of the three examples used above to illustrate the complex
sentence lend themselves naturally to this use of participles:

2. *Following the trail,* we found ourselves on an exposed hillside.
3. We looked for a snug spot, out of the wind, *having brought no
   jackets.*

But the first sentence does not lend itself as well to this usage. It contains
an "adversative" clause, with "although," and in English we like to see
any adversative element plainly stated. We would probably *not* say:

1. The sun being warm, the wind was chilly.

But Greek would feel no difficulty about this kind of construction. So
in translating into English, one is often forced to make explicit what is
only implicit in the Greek sentence.

In summary, much of the time it is possible to translate a Greek
participle with an English participle. When that proves clumsy, however,
or even impossible, remember that there is a convenient rule of thumb
that will help you to resolve the question of meaning: If the participle
has a definite article with it, try translating it with an English relative
clause; if it does not, try translating it with an English adverbial clause
— even if you have to use "although" or "if" as the subordinating
conjunction.*

γ′ ΕΞΗΓΗΤΙΚΑ

Basic Books for an Exegetical Library

Anyone who will be called on to offer leadership in a Christian community needs to be able to work exegetically with the Scriptures. The

---

* There are exceptions to this rule, arising from the fact that the earliest forms of literary
Greek (those of the Homeric age) had no article at all. The continuing influence of
Homeric language was such that it was always possible, when a later writer was being
solemn, to omit articles. Luke, for example, does this in the Magnificat (Luke 1:53).
As a result, absence of the article does not *always* imply that the participial phrase is
the equivalent of an adverbial clause.

objective of such exegesis may be preaching or teaching, or one's primary purpose may be simply to grow in understanding the gospel — growth that will inevitably affect us and our communities, perhaps in unforeseen ways. The methods of exegesis help us set aside, to some degree, our own preoccupations and presuppositions about the meaning of Scripture and hear afresh the words of our text as words written by real people for real people — but people of another place and time, another culture and language.

No one can do exegesis very well in isolation. None of us is smart enough or broadly educated enough to catch the full range of possible meanings. And probably none of us is self-critical enough always to notice when we are riding our own hobbyhorses rather than doing real exegesis. Accordingly, we need to be in conversation with other exegetes — in person, where that is possible, and also through the writings of those for whom exegesis is their life vocation. For this reason, access to some sort of exegetical library is essential for anyone who wants to study Scripture seriously.

No exegete, no matter how famous, is going to be correct all the time. Accordingly, there is no one book that will settle all arguments or uncertainties — and no one book or series of books that will make for a complete or finished exegetical library. Sometimes it is very difficult to decide among what is available. Here are some suggestions:

For the text of the New Testament:

> *The Greek New Testament,* ed. K. Aland, M. Black, C. M. Martini, B. M. Metzger, and A. W. Wikgren (3rd ed. [corrected]; New York: United Bible Societies, 1983). This text, which you have been using, is the best available at present for the average student of the Greek New Testament.

> B. M. Metzger, *A Textual Commentary on the Greek New Testament.* New York: United Bible Societies, 1971. This volume is the companion to *The Greek New Testament* and explains how the editors made their decisions as to the correct text.

> An interlinear Greek-English New Testament may also be useful for occasional reference, but the translation will tend to dominate your reading of the Greek and may deprive you of some of the advantage of encountering the text on your own.

To aid in study of the words of the New Testament:

> W. Bauer, *A Greek-English Lexicon of the New Testament and Other Early Christian Literature,* tr. and adapted by W. F. Arndt, F. W. Gingrich, and F. W. Danker (2nd ed.; Chicago: University of Chicago, 1979). This lexicon, which you have been using, is the best available. The *Greek-English Lexicon of the New Testament Based on Semantic Domains,* ed. J. P. Louw and E. A. Nida (2 vols.; New York: United Bible Societies, 1988) brings together words of related meanings and so can be helpful in study of concepts that go beyond single words.

> R. E. Van Voorst, *Building Your New Testament Greek Vocabulary* (Grand Rapids: Eerdmans, 1990). To help you gain better command of Greek vocabulary, this volume groups words according to their frequency in the New Testament and in groups of cognates.

> *Theological Dictionary of the New Testament,* ed. G. Kittel and G. Friedrich, tr. G. W. Bromiley (10 vols.; Grand Rapids: Eerdmans, 1964-76). This big set of tomes is full of interesting information about the background of the New Testament vocabulary in both Gentile and Jewish literature. Sometimes the conclusions of the different authors involved are facile. Still, the volumes are full of useful information. A one-volume abridgment is also available. A similar work on a smaller scale (three large volumes) and more up-to-date is the *Exegetical Dictionary of the New Testament,* ed. H. Balz and G. Schneider (Grand Rapids: Eerdmans, 1990-93).

> *The Eerdmans Analytical Concordance to the Revised Standard Version of the Bible,* compiled by R. E. Whitaker (Grand Rapids: Eerdmans, 1988). This concordance (or one of the older ones by R. Young or J. Strong and based on the King James Version) will be useful. Concordances that do not tell you about the Greek (and Hebrew and Aramaic) behind the English are not much more than fancy indexes to a particular English translation.

To aid in study of the grammar of the New Testament:

>   F. Blass and A. Debrunner, *A Greek Grammar of the New Testament and Other Early Christian Literature,* tr. and revised R. W. Funk (Chicago: University of Chicago, 1961). This is the standard grammar of New Testament language in English. It is somewhat difficult to use as a normal grammar, but the index can guide you to useful material relating to a particular text. Another large-scale grammar was initiated by J. H. Moulton and continued by W. F. Howard and N. Turner, *A Grammar of New Testament Greek* (4 vols.; Edinburgh: T. & T. Clark, 1906-76).

>   C. F. D. Moule, *An Idiom-Book of New Testament Greek* (2nd ed.; Cambridge: Cambridge University Press, 1971). A useful collection of observations about the way Greek does things. The index makes it possible to look up any passage you may be working on to see if there are useful notes here.

Bible dictionaries:

>   *Harper's Bible Dictionary,* ed. P. J. Achtemeier (San Francisco: Harper and Row, 1985). This is a very good and up-to-date one-volume dictionary. (It replaced an earlier and less comprehensive work with the same title, so take note of the year of publication if you buy a used copy.)

>   *The Interpreter's Dictionary of the Bible,* ed. G. A. Buttrick, et al. (4 vols.; Nashville: Abingdon, 1962); supplementary volume, ed. K. Crim (Nashville: Abingdon, 1976). This is a very good multi-volume Bible dictionary and an excellent resource on most biblical subjects. The supplementary volume brings many important topics up to date.

>   *The Anchor Bible Dictionary,* ed. D. N. Freedman (6 vols.; Garden City, NY: Doubleday, 1992). Very up-to-date. Another multi-volume dictionary, which generally represents more conservative approaches and conclusions, is the *International Standard Bible Encyclopedia,* revised edition ed. G. W. Bromiley, et al. (4 vols., 1979-88).

Bible commentaries:

A good *one-volume* Bible commentary is important for ready reference. Two that can be recommended are *Harper's Bible Commentary,* ed. J. L. Mays (San Francisco: Harper and Row, 1988), and *The New Jerome Biblical Commentary,* ed. R. E. Brown, J. A. Fitzmyer, and R. E. Murphy (New York: Paulist, 1989).

There is no single *series* of commentaries that is absolutely predictable. In general, a person who can read some Greek and wants a well-qualified companion to share the process of exegesis will find that these series are fairly reliable:

The New Century Bible (a very capable British series, published in the U.S. by Eerdmans),

Black's / Harper's New Testament Commentaries (some but not all of these volumes, published in the U.K. by A. & C. Black, have been published in the U.S. by Harper and Row),

Westminster-Pelican Commentaries (another British series published by an American publisher),

Hermeneia (a more demanding, academic-oriented series of commentaries being published by Fortress),

The Anchor Bible (an uneven series with many excellent individual volumes, published by Doubleday), and

TPI New Testament Commentaries (a new and accessible series being published jointly by SCM and Trinity Press International).

Some good individual volumes *based specifically on the Greek text are:*

F. W. Beare, *The Gospel According to Matthew: A Commentary* (Oxford: Basil Blackwell, 1981).

C. E. B. Cranfield, *The Gospel According to St. Mark* (Cambridge: Cambridge University Press, 1959), in the Cambridge Greek Testament Commentaries series.

V. Taylor, *The Gospel According to St. Mark* (2nd ed.; New York: St. Martin's, 1968).

I. H. Marshall, *The Gospel of Luke: A Commentary on the Greek Text* (Grand Rapids: Eerdmans, 1978), in the New International Greek Testament Commentary series.

C. K. Barrett, *The Gospel According to St. John* (2nd ed.; Philadelphia: Westminster, 1978).

E. Haenchen, *The Acts of the Apostles: A Commentary* (Philadelphia: Westminster, 1971).

E. Käsemann, *Commentary on Romans,* tr. G. W. Bromiley (Grand Rapids: Eerdmans, 1980).

LESSON XXIII

α' ΛΕΞΙΣ 1 John 5:18-21

5:18 γεγεννημένος . . . γεννηθεὶς What tenses are these participles? Are they meant to convey different meanings, or are both simply functioning as "past" participles, carrying essentially the same information? To whom do they refer?

αὐτόν Who or what is the antecedent of this pronoun? What does the clause mean? Do you see signs in n. 7 of the textual apparatus that others may have been puzzled by it? What would the clause mean if you accepted the reading ἑαυτόν? The reflexives (such as ἑαυτόν) may at one time have existed also in a contracted form, αὑτόν. The early uncials simply read AYTON, with no breathing mark, and could therefore have been referring to either αὑτόν or αὐτόν. Which variant do you think is more in tune with the thought of the letter?

+ἅπτεται see Bauer s.v. ἅπτω, but read carefully! The active and middle voices have quite different meanings. When Bauer tells you that the middle voice means "touch, take hold of, hold τινός someone or someth.," that is its way of telling you that the verb takes its object in the genitive case.

5:19 +ὅλος see Bauer

+κεῖται see Bauer s.v. κεῖμαι: definition 2.d has some suggestions about this verse

158

5:20 +ἥκει   see Bauer

διάνοιαν   see Bauer

+ἀληθινόν   see Bauer and compare the related adjective
ἀληθής You can see from the textual apparatus that some scribes
found this phrase odd and wanted more specificity. Therefore, they
either added θεόν or changed the gender to τὸ ἀληθινόν, *the truth*
(neuter adjectives with the article are often used as abstract nouns).
The phrase ἐν τῷ ἀληθινῷ suggests that ὁ ἀληθινός is the opposite
of ὁ πονηρός in v. 19.

5:21 +εἰδώλων   see Bauer

β′ ΓΡΑΜΜΑΤΙΚΑ

The Genitive Absolute

Here are some examples of the "absolute" construction in English:

- *The President having fainted during an orientation lecture,* the Dean
  rushed out to find a doctor.
- *The doctor being a podiatrist,* we despaired of her ability to help.
- *His collar having been loosened,* some color began to return to the
  President's face.
- *He being able to speak again,* the doctor asked him how he felt.
- *She disbelieving what he said,* he became petulant.
- *His collar being handed back to him,* he threw it down and stamped
  on it, claiming that it had throttled him.

Not exactly the preferred way of writing a narrative in English, is it?
Still, we do have an "absolute" construction and we do use it occasionally
in relatively formal English, for example, in laudatory addresses: "Today
being the fiftieth anniversary of the founding of the Emmeline and
Heribert Waldvogel Home for Foundling Dachshunds, we are gathered
to honor the generosity, etc." Though it is odd to find it in other contexts,
we can understand what is being said.

What, then, is an absolute construction? It is a kind of subordinate clause that hangs in the air. Its verb is a participle, and its subject is some person or thing other than the subject of the main verb in the sentence. In English, if you absolutely have to use a pronoun for the subject of an absolute, it is supposed to be in the nominative case. You juxtapose the whole construction with an otherwise normal-seeming sentence, but leave it without any grammatical connection to the rest of the sentence. The absolute construction merely tells the listener to keep certain information in mind and momentarily suspend judgment on its significance or its relation to the rest of the sentence.

The differences between the absolute construction in English and in Hellenistic Greek are (1) that we put ours in the nominative case while they put theirs in the genitive and (2) that they used the absolute construction more. You have not seen any examples of it in 1 John, which is not surprising, since the syntax of 1 John is very simple, on the whole, and just a bit Semitic (meaning that it omits some of the more idiomatic Greek ways of doing things). Elsewhere in the New Testament, however, the genitive absolute is a fairly common construction. Some examples for study:

Καὶ ἐκπορευομένου αὐτοῦ εἰς ὁδὸν προσδραμὼν εἷς καὶ γονυπετήσας αὐτὸν ἐπηρώτα αυτόν, Διδάσκαλε ἀγαθέ, τί ποιήσω ἵνα ζωὴν αἰώνιον κληρονομήσω;

And, *he coming out into the road,* a certain person, having run up and knelt down to him, asked him, "Good teacher, what shall I do to inherit eternal life?" (Mark 10:17)

A smoother English translation of this would be: "As he was coming out into the road, a certain person. . . ."

Καὶ ὄντος τοῦ Πέτρου κάτω ἐν τῇ αὐλῇ ἔρχεται μία τῶν παιδισκῶν τοῦ ἀρχιερέως, καὶ ἰδοῦσα τὸν Πέτρον . . . λέγει, Καὶ σὺ μετὰ τοῦ Ναζαρηνοῦ ἦσθα τοῦ Ἰησοῦ.

And, *Peter being downstairs in the courtyard,* one of the high priest's maids comes and, seeing Peter . . . , says, "You were with the Nazarene, too — [with] Jesus." (Mark 14:66-67)

A translation in better English would be: "While Peter was downstairs in the courtyard, one of the high priest's maids. . . ."

Ἔτι λαλοῦντος τοῦ Πέτρου τὰ ῥήματα ταῦτα ἐπέπεσεν τὸ πνεῦμα τὸ ἅγιον ἐπὶ πάντας τοὺς ἀκούοντας τὸν λόγον.

Peter still speaking these words, the Holy Spirit fell upon all those hearing the speech. (Acts 10:44)

A smoother translation would be: "While Peter was still speaking these words, the Holy Spirit. . . ."

Φοβηθῶμεν οὖν μήποτε καταλειπομένης ἐπαγγελίας εἰσελθεῖν εἰς τὴν κατάπαυσιν αὐτοῦ δοκῇ τις ἐξ ὑμῶν ὑστερηκέναι

Let us fear, then, lest, *[the] promise of entering into his rest being left behind,* some one from among you may seem to have fallen short. (Heb. 4:1)

Or better: "Let us fear, then, lest, if the promise of entering into his rest is left behind, some one from among you. . . ."

While the ease with which Greek used the genitive absolute may be a little confusing to speakers of English, the construction itself is basically familiar to us. Once you have identified what it is, you can experiment to find a felicitous translation.

γ΄ ΕΞΗΓΗΤΙΚΑ

Some Concluding Remarks on Exegesis

In the final analysis, exegesis is nothing more or less than good Bible study. The goal of reading and studying the Bible is to let the biblical authors speak to us. Some may prefer to say "to let God speak to us through the biblical authors." I have no quarrel with that way of stating it, either — so long as we remember that it is really a matter of God speaking through particular historical authors. God has other ways, too, of speaking to human beings, but the specific value of the Scriptures is that they also involve us in dialogue with associates in faith from far-distant centuries, people who may have seen the world very differently and who can help us perceive and admit the incompleteness and relativity of our own presuppositions.

This means that exegesis involves us in three basic tasks: The first is the task of *gathering information,* of acquiring knowledge about the world in which the biblical authors wrote, including their languages and the cultures which defined their understanding of the world. That is what you have been working toward in this course: gaining better knowledge of the Greek language and, implicitly, the first-century Mediterranean culture it conveyed. This is a task that no modern person, by definition, can ever complete, since we can never truly get "inside" the first century. But all that we can learn will help us get closer and form a truer conception of the context of our texts.

The second task is that of *engaging with the text itself.* The text that we are trying to understand deserves at least as much focused attention as a good friend who is telling us something of importance. We should expect to be surprised, sometimes, by what we are told. And we should expect that at times we will have a hard time understanding the text. One of the delights of exegesis, in fact, is that one can return over and over again in one's lifetime to the same text and discover aspects of it that went unnoticed before — perhaps even whole new ranges of meaning in the text. What you have studied in these lessons will help you engage with the text. But you also need to cultivate the human and spiritual gift of paying attention — the same attention we need to give to one another as well.

The third task is that of *exercising judgment.* This means — to use another valuable phrase for it — "being critical." We should behave critically toward the text itself by expecting it to mean something of importance and refusing to accept half-formed, biased, automatic, or sentimental interpretations. We should be equally critical of ourselves by demanding that our own insights and ideas stand the test of comparison with the text. Yes, I may just have had a wonderful idea about the real meaning of Mark 1:1, and I may be quite overwhelmed with both the intellectual cleverness and the spiritual profundity of my interpretation. But let me take it back to the text and test it there. If my interpretation is right, if this is really what Mark meant — then he should not have contradicted it five verses further on. He should have said it in some reasonably forthright way — not using language that, on careful reading, says the exact opposite. He ought to have given hints elsewhere in his book that my interpretation is an appropriate way of approaching the matter. If I am self-critical, I will be ready to throw out even ideas that I was quite stuck on if they do not seem to hold up to being tested. As one goes along in the practice of exegesis, one learns more about ways of testing ideas. But this is primarily a matter not of technique but of personal honesty. What one most needs to develop is the ability to find oneself wrong!

To do exegesis well requires us to pursue all three of these tasks with some energy: acquiring knowledge, engaging with the text, exercising critical judgment. They are not sequential in the sense that you have to finish (or could ever finish) with one before going on to the next. Instead, they go hand in hand. New knowledge may allow you to read a text in a new sense or to test a new hypothesis. A new reading of the text may cause you to question what you thought you knew. The reluctant recognition that a favorite sermon of yours did not really reflect the text on which you were preaching may open the door to a whole new range of meaning — and to a sense of where you need new knowledge, too.

Exegesis is not a project that can ever be finished. It is the enjoyment of a friendship that never wears out. Any friendship requires your active involvement in order to stay alive and healthy. Exegesis is the way in which you ensure that your relationship with Scripture stays alive and healthy and can continue to surprise you with good news.

LESSON XXIV

α′ ΛΕΞΙΣ 2 John

1   +πρεσβύτερος   *elder;* what English derivatives do you know?

+ἐκλεκτῇ   see Bauer

+κυρία   the feminine equivalent of κύριος, used as a respectful form of address

+μόνος   see Bauer; what English derivatives do you know?

2   ἔσται   a form of the verb εἰμί; see p. 186 if it is hard to place

3   +χάρις   see Bauer   This is one of the great theological words of the New Testament; it is a 3rd declension fem. noun. The gen. sg. is χάριτος, but it has the peculiar acc. sg. χάριν.

+ἔλεος   another of the great theological words

+εἰρήνη   and another

+παρά   a preposition; with gen. it means *from*

4   +ἐχάρην   the irregular aorist of χαίρω; see Bauer   Notice in part 2 of the lexicon article that this verb supplied the normal formulas of greeting in Hellenistic Greek (the functional equivalent of "hello") in the form of imperatives: χαῖρε, χαίρετε (literally, *rejoice!*). There is a play on this usage at the end of 2 John.

+λίαν   see Bauer

+εὕρηκα   See the list of irregular verbs under εὑρίσκω. In Latinized form, this word is the motto of the state of California.

+περιπατοῦντας   literally, *walking* This is not a normal Greek idiom, but a translation of a Hebrew idiom meaning *living, behaving, conducting [oneself]*.

ἐλάβομεν   See the list of irregular verbs under λαμβάνω, which we have encountered earlier. Familiarize yourself with this verb, as other forms (including a compound) will appear in this letter.

5   +καινήν   see Bauer

6   ἠκούσατε   if you have trouble finding this verb, remember that η can be the augmented form of α

7   +πλάνοι   see Bauer; this is related to πλανάω, which you have already learned

ἐξῆλθον   if this seems puzzling, see the list of irregular verbs under ἔρχομαι

8   +ἀπολέσητε   see the list of irregular verbs under ἀπόλλυμι Since this is an aorist subjunctive form, the augmented <u>ω</u> in aorist indicative forms such as ἀπώλεσα has gone back to the basic o of the stem. This verb gives us the name of an important demon: Apollyon, the Destroyer.

+εἰργασάμεθα   see Bauer, remembering to discount the augment.   When a stem ending in ζ has to add a -σ- infix, it drops the ζ. Notice the confusion between "we" and "you" in this verse, as indicated by the textual apparatus.

+μισθόν   see Bauer

+πλήρη   *full*; the lexicon form is πλήρης; this is masc. acc. sg., contracted from πλήρεα

ἀπολάβητε   from ἀπολαμβάνω

9   προάγω   *going ahead*; perhaps, in this context, *going too far*

+διδαχῇ   *teaching*; related to the verb διδάσκω, which we have met

10   +φέρει   the irregular verb φέρω means *bring, bear, carry*

+οἰκίαν   see Bauer

+χαίρειν αὐτῷ μὴ λέγετε   *Do not tell him hello* Literally: *Do not tell him to rejoice.* Notice how the next verse repeats this phrase with variation.

11   κοινωνεῖ   *shares in* (with dat.); from the verb κοινωνέω, which is related to κοινωνία

12   +ἐβουλήθην   see the list of irregular verbs under βούλομαι

διὰ χάρτου καὶ μέλανος   *with (by means of) paper and ink*

ἐλπίζω   a verb related to ἐλπίς, which you have already met

στόμα πρὸς στόμα   an idiom meaning what we mean by *face to face;* literally: *mouth to mouth*

λαλῆσαι   aor. act. inf. of λαλέω, *to speak* This verb is one of the roots of the English word "glossolalia."

+πεπληρωμένη   perf. pass. participle of πληρόω, which is related to πλήρης (v. 8)   Can you guess the meaning of this verbal form before you look it up?

13   +ἀσπάζεται   see Bauer

ἀδελφῆς   ἀδελφή is the feminine equivalent of ἀδελφός

β΄ ΓΡΑΜΜΑΤΙΚΑ

A Further Use of the Infinitive

Another use of the infinitive, not previously discussed, is the "articular infinitive." Although this usage is not found in the Johannine letters, it is moderately common in other New Testament writings and is included here, in our final grammatical discussion, for completeness and for future reference.

Infinitives function not only as verbs, but as nouns. This is true in English as well as Greek:

To study Greek is a privilege and gives us power *to understand* the New Testament better.

In this sentence, "to study" is a noun serving as the subject of "is," with "privilege" as predicate nominative. "To understand" is a noun in apposition to "power." That is, it specifies more exactly what sort of "power" is meant. (Cf. such expressions as "Charles, my uncle" or "My friend Ruth," where "uncle" and "Ruth" are in apposition to "Charles" and "friend.")

In English, however, we have another kind of verbal noun that we are, on the whole, more comfortable with: the gerund. The form of the gerund is the same as that of the present active participle:

infinitive	gerund
to sing	singing
to study	studying
to be	being
to run	running

The example sentence from the previous paragraph could be rewritten with gerunds:

Studying Greek is a privilege and gives us the power of understanding the New Testament better.

The meaning is the same, but the gerund, especially as subject, is more idiomatic in English.

Greek had nothing equivalent to our gerund. The infinitive was its only verbal noun and was used quite broadly. It was also common to use the definite article with the infinitive in order to help ear and eye distinguish when it was being used strictly as a noun rather than in indirect discourse or as complement to another verb (cf. above, Lesson XVII). In English you cannot really say "the to study." But in Greek, it was quite normal to say τὸ μανθάνειν, and that is how the opening of our example sentence would have to be translated into Greek. (Notice that infinitives are considered neuter in gender.)

The "articular infinitive" (i.e., the infinitive with the article) was a highly flexible grammatical device that could be used in ways that have little parallel in English. Since it is moderately common in the New Testament, it will be a good idea to offer a few examples here. An articular infinitive may serve as *direct object:*

ζηλοῦτε τὸ προφητεύειν, καὶ τὸ λαλεῖν μὴ κωλύετε γλώσσαις

Be zealous for *prophesying,* and do not prohibit *speaking* in tongues. (1 Cor. 14:39)

An articular infinitive may also serve as the *object of a preposition:*

Φίλιππος . . . εὐηγγελίζετο τὰς πόλεις πάσας ἕως τοῦ ἐλθεῖν αὐτὸν εἰς Καισάρειαν

Philip . . . evangelized all the cities until his *coming* into Caesarea. (Acts 8:40)

In this last case, the infinitive is in the genitive because that is the case that ἕως governs. (The form of the infinitive itself never changes; only the article tells us the case.) And this infinitive has a subject (αὐτόν), which is in the accusative case — the norm for all subjects of infinitives in Greek. In English, a gerund cannot take a subject, but it can be modified by a possessive, giving the same general idea. Here is a similar example:

. . . οἷς καὶ παρέστησεν ἑαυτὸν ζῶντα μετὰ τὸ παθεῖν αὐτὸν ἐν πολλοῖς τεκμηρίοις . . .

. . . to whom, also, he presented himself alive after his *suffering* by means of many demonstrations. . . . (Acts 1:3)

Some uses of the articular infinitive can hardly be translated into English in word-for-word fashion. They must simply be accepted as "idioms" and replaced by equivalent English idioms. But they operate in the same way as the examples you have just looked at; the problem is just that English usage is not flexible enough to accommodate them. For example, Greek used the preposition ἐν with an articular infinitive to indicate that an action takes place *when* or *while* another action (expressed in the infinitive) is happening:

Καὶ ἐν τῷ <u>συμπληροῦσθαι</u> τὴν ἡμέραν τῆς πεντηκοστῆς ἦσαν πάντες ὁμοῦ ἐπὶ τὸ αὐτό

And when the day of Pentecost *came round,* they were all together at the same place. (Acts 2:1)

ἐν δὲ τῷ <u>πορεύεσθαι</u> ἐγένετο αὐτὸν ἐγγίζειν τῇ Δαμασκῷ . . .

And while [he] was *traveling,* it came to pass that he neared Damascus. . . . (Acts 9:3)

In the second example, ἐγγίζειν is also an infinitive and is used in a form of indirect discourse after ἐγένετο. Ἐγένετο with an infinitive, like "it came to pass that . . ." in English, is an imitation of Hebrew grammar.

Perhaps most confusing for the English-speaking person is the use of the articular infinitive to express *purpose.* This could be done in two ways, either by using the preposition εἰς with the infinitive in the accusative or by using the articular infinitive by itself in the genitive case. Here are some examples:

. . . ἐζήτουν κατὰ τοῦ Ἰησοῦ μαρτυρίαν εἰς <u>τὸ θανατῶσαι</u> αὐτόν . . .

. . . they were seeking evidence against Jesus in order *to execute* him. . . . (Mark 14:55)

ἐπιποθῶ γὰρ ἰδεῖν ὑμᾶς, ἵνα τι μεταδῶ χάρισμα ὑμῖν πνευματικὸν εἰς <u>τὸ στηριχθῆναι</u> ὑμᾶς . . .

For I want to see you so that I may share some spiritual gift with you in order for you *to be strengthened.* . . . (Rom. 1:11)

καὶ σημεῖον ἔλαβεν περιτομῆς, σφραγῖδα τῆς δικαιοσύνης τῆς πίστεως τῆς ἐν τῇ ἀκροβυστίᾳ, εἰς <u>τὸ εἶναι</u> αὐτὸν πατέρα πάντων τῶν πιστευόντων δι᾽ ἀκροβυστίας, εἰς <u>τὸ λογισθῆναι</u> αὐτοῖς δικαιοσύνην . . .

And [Abraham] received the sign of circumcision, seal of the righteousness of the faith that [he had] in uncircumcision, in order for him *to be* father of all who believe while uncircumcised, so that righteousness *might be reckoned* to them. . . . (Rom. 4:11)

καὶ ἐν τῷ <u>εἰσαγαγεῖν</u> τοὺς γονεῖς τὸ παιδίον Ἰησοῦν τοῦ ποιῆσαι αὐτοὺς κατὰ τὸ εἰθισμένον τοῦ νόμου περὶ αὐτοῦ καὶ αὐτὸς ἐδέξατο αὐτὸ εἰς τὰς ἀγκάλας. . . .

And when the parents *brought* the child Jesus so that they *might do* for him according to the custom of the law, he [Simeon], too, took him into his arms. . . . (Luke 2:27f.)

You do not need to know anything about *articular infinitives* in order to read 1, 2, or 3 John. But for much of the rest of the New Testament they are important. Accordingly, it is worthwhile to study the explanations and examples above carefully — and unnecessary to work up high anxiety about them! As for infinitives in *indirect discourse* and as *complements* of other verbs, you have already encountered them and they do not pose many problems for those familiar with English.

EXERCISES

Translate the following sentences into English. Their vocabulary is drawn from previous lessons.

α΄ ἐν τῷ ἀγαπᾶν τοὺς ἀδελφούς, μένετε ἐν τῷ λόγῳ μου.

β΄ θέλω ὑμᾶς, τεκνία, γινώσκειν τὴν ἐντολὴν ταύτην εἰς τὸ μὴ ἁμαρτάνειν ὑμᾶς.

γ΄ μετὰ τὸ γράφειν ἡμῖν, ἔμεινε μετ᾽ αὐτῶν.

δ΄ Ἰησοῦς ἦλθε τοῦ γινώσκειν ὑμᾶς πάντα.

ε΄ μετὰ τὸ τελειοῦσθαι τὸν κόσμον, ὁμολογήσομεν τὸν θεὸν καὶ τὸν χριστὸν αὐτοῦ εἰς τὸν αἰῶνα.

LESSON XXV

ΛΕΞΙΣ α´ 3 John

2 **+εὔχομαι** see Bauer and be sure to check all definitions; the two infinitives that follow are in indirect discourse

+εὐοδοῦσθαι contracted from [εὐοδόεσθαι]; see Bauer

ὑγιαίνειν see Bauer

3 **ἐρχομένων ἀδελφῶν καὶ μαρτυρούντων . . .** a genitive absolute! cf. Lesson XXIII; for the dative with μαρτυρέω, see Bauer s.v. 1.c

4 **μειζοτέραν** μείζων already means "greater," but the popular language apparently doubled the comparison into μειζότερος (adding on the regular comparative ending -οτερος) — rather like saying "more bigger" in English.

χαράν *joy*; note the variant reading χάριν

5 **πιστὸν** *faithful,* related to πίστις and πιστεύω

καὶ τοῦτο +ξένους This phrase is equivalent to English idiomatic *and strangers at that.* ξένος is the source of our word "xenophobia."

6 **ἐνώπιον** *in the presence of,* a preposition with genitive

+ἐκκλησίας See Bauer, though you may well know this word

171

already. It originally referred to the *assembly* of the citizen body
of a city or tribe.

οὓς   the antecedent is ἀδελφοὺς in v. 5; accusative as the object
of προπέμψας

+καλῶς   an adverb with the typical -ως ending, derived from
καλός; see Bauer

+προπέμψας   *having sent . . . on,* aorist active participle of προ-
πέμπω

+ἀξίως   adverb related to ἄξιος; see Bauer

7   +ἐθνικῶν   see Bauer; related to ἔθνος, ἔθνους (nom. pl. ἔθνη),
nation, which is more often the term for *gentiles*

8   ὑπολαμβάνειν   see Bauer

τοὺς τοιούτους   *such persons;* see Bauer, s.v. τοιοῦτος, τοιαύτη,
τοιοῦτον   Except for the neuter nom. and acc. sg., which end in
ν, this demonstrative is declined like οὗτος, αὕτη, τοῦτο.

συνεργοὶ   συν- is equivalent to the element *co-* / *con-* in Latin-
derived words. The root εργ- (as in ἔργον or ἐργάζομαι) has to
do with *work.* Therefore, this word means *co-workers.*

9   ἔγραψα τι τῇ ἐκκλησίᾳ   Note the variant readings that include
the expression ἔγραψα ἄν, meaning *I would have written.* The
particle ἄν, when used with an indicative verb, implies that the
statement is contrary to fact.

φιλοπρωτεύων   see Bauer, and note the uncertainty about the
exact meaning

ἐπιδέχεται   see Bauer; hospitality was a fundamental Christian
duty

10   ἔλθω   subjunctive of ἦλθον

+ὑπομνήσω   see Bauer s.v. ὑπομιμνήσκω   A few O-verbs
share the iota-reduplication in the present system that is found in
MI-verbs such as δίδωμι and τίθημι.

φλυαρῶν   see Bauer

ἀρκούμενος This form is contracted from [ἀρκεόμενος]. See Bauer, noting that the meaning of the passive is a little different from that of the active.

+κωλύει   see Bauer

+ἐκβάλλει   see Bauer, and note that the verb normally has a strong force

11 +μιμοῦ   see Bauer, s.v. μιμέομαι: the opening paragraph explains this form; cf. English "mime"

+κακόν   see Bauer

+ἀγαθόν   see Bauer

ἀγαθοποιῶν You can probably figure out the meaning of this verb from its component parts: ἀγαθός and ποιέω.

κακοποιῶν   cf. the preceding note

12 Δημητρίῳ μεμαρτύρηται This construction is perplexing from an English point of view, but the lexicon explains it fairly clearly (s.v. μαρτυρέω 2.b).

ὑπὸ πάντων, κ.τ.λ.   With passive verbs, ὑπό indicates the agent: "Good testimony is given to Demetrius *by* all and *by*. . . ."

αὐτῆς τῆς ἀληθείας   αὐτῆς here in its intensive function: *itself*

13 διὰ μέλανος καὶ καλάμου   *with ink and pen;* cf. 2 John 12

14 εὐθέως   an adverb: *soon, quickly*

ἰδεῖν   infinitive of εἶδον

στόμα πρὸς στόμα   see note above on 2 John 12

15 +φίλοι   see Bauer

κατ' ὄνομα   *by (according to) name*

ΛΕΞΙΣ β′   John 1:1-18
(The Prologue of John's Gospel)

1:1   ἦν   if this looks unfamiliar, see p. 186

πρὸς   With acc. this preposition normally means *to, toward*. But when the associated verb contains no sense of motion, it means *with, in the presence of.*

θεὸς ἦν ὁ λόγος   Here λόγος is the subject and θεὸς is the predicate nominative. In linking-verb sentences, the subject is often "marked" by the definite article, while the predicate nominative is anarthrous.

1:3   πάντα . . . ἐγένετο   Remember that neuter pl. subjects typically take sg. verbs. The basic meaning of γίνομαι is *become,* but it can also mean *come to be, happen, turn out to be.*

+χωρὶς   see Bauer

οὐδὲ ἕν   οὐδὲ is the conjunction / adverb *nor, not even.* If ἕν seems unfamiliar, see p. 184. The note in the textual apparatus reveals an ancient and long-standing uncertainty as to the correct punctuation here. Does the period belong after ἕν or after γέγονεν?

1:5   φαίνει   see Bauer; the word is more common in the passive, with a different meaning

κατέλαβεν   λαβ- is the aorist stem of λαμβάνω. See κατα-λαμβάνω in Bauer and note carefully the range of meanings: More than one might be appropriate here, and we might even be looking at a deliberate play on words.

1:6   ἀπεσταλμένος   if this seems unfamiliar, look at the chart of irregular verbs

ὄνομα αὐτῷ   *his name;* the dative can express possession, though that is more often the task of the genitive

1:7   εἰς μαρτυρίαν   εἰς can express purpose, as we saw in the discussion of the articular infinitive in the preceding lesson

πιστεύσωσιν   aorist subj., implying that the goal is that all should *come* to believe, rather than *go on* believing (which would be expressed with present subj.)

1:8 ἀλλ' ἵνα μαρτυρήσῃ   something like ἦλθεν, *he came*, is implied after ἀλλ'

1:9 +φωτίζει   see Bauer

πάντα   it may look neut. pl., but it is not; see p. 184 if you are uncertain

1:10 ἔγνω   if it seems unfamiliar, try under γινώσκω

1:11 +ἴδια . . . ἴδιοι   see Bauer and note carefully the difference of genders

+παρέλαβον   see Bauer; cf. κατέλαβεν in v. 5

1:12 +ὅσοι   see Bauer

+ἐξουσίαν   see Bauer; this noun often takes, as here, a complementary infinitive

τοῖς πιστεύουσιν εἰς . . .   πιστεύω εἰς is a favorite Johannine expression, which we translate, perhaps inadequately, *believe in*. πιστεύουσιν here is in apposition to αὐτοῖς.

1:13 αἱμάτων The plural is odd. It apparently signifies "flows of blood," i.e., the menstrual flow

+ἀνδρὸς   see Bauer s.v. ἀνήρ and note the full range of meanings

1:14 ἐσκήνωσεν   see Bauer

ἐν ἡμῖν   *among us;* ἐν typically means *among* with a pl. object

1:15 +κέκραγεν   see Bauer s.v. κράζω

Ὁ ὀπίσω μου ἐρχόμενος   *the one coming after me* It is not unusual for article and substantive to be separated like this in order to sandwich some important modifier between them.

+ἔμπροσθεν   see Bauer

πρῶτός μου   Literally, *first than me*. The genitive is used with comparative and superlative adjectives (and "first" is practically a superlative) to define the nature of the comparison (see Lesson XV).

1:16 +πληρώματος   see Bauer   This was a favorite Gnostic word, but it was also important among orthodox Christian writers.

χάριν ἀντὶ χάριτος   a difficult phrase; for some discussion of it, see Bauer s.v. ἀντί

1:17 +νόμος   see Bauer

ἐδόθη   aorist passive of δίδωμι

1:18 ὁ +ὤν   participle of εἰμί; cf. p. 185

εἰς τὸν κόλπον   ἐν τῷ κόλπῳ might have seemed more likely, but John likes to use prepositions implying motion with verbs that do not. Cf. his use of πρός with ἦν in vv. 1-2.

+ἐξηγήσατο   see Bauer; this is the verb related to our noun "exegesis"

PARADIGMS

I. Substantives

A. Nouns of the First Declension

1. Feminine *nouns show some variation between* α *and* η *endings in the singular:*

ἀγγελία, -ας, ἡ, *message*

	sg.	pl.
nom.	ἀγγελία	ἀγγελίαι
gen.	ἀγγελίας	ἀγγελιῶν
dat.	ἀγγελίᾳ	ἀγγελίαις
acc.	ἀγγελίαν	ἀγγελίας

ἀρχή, -ῆς, ἡ, *beginning, rule*

	sg.	pl.
nom.	ἀρχή	ἀρχαί
gen.	ἀρχῆς	ἀρχῶν
dat.	ἀρχῇ	ἀρχαῖς
acc.	ἀρχήν	ἀρχάς

δόξα, -ης, ἡ, *reputation, glory*

	sg.	pl.
gen.	δόξα	δόξαι
nom.	δόξης	δοξῶν
dat.	δόξῃ	δόξαις
acc.	δόξαν	δόξας

2. First declension masculine *nouns differ from the feminine nouns only in nom. and gen. sg.:*

νεανίας, -ου, ὁ, *youth, young man*

	sg.	pl.
nom.	νεανίας	νεανίαι
gen.	νεανίου	νεανιῶν
dat.	νεανίῃ	νεανίαις
acc.	νεανίαν	νεανίας

μαθητής, -οῦ, ὁ, *disciple*

	sg.	pl.
nom.	μαθητής	μαθηταί
gen.	μαθητοῦ	μαθητῶν
dat.	μαθητῇ	μαθηταῖς
acc.	μαθητήν	μαθητάς

B. Nouns of the Second Declension

1. Masculine *and* feminine *use exactly the same endings:*

λόγος, -ου, ὁ, *word, speech* (masc.)

	sg.	pl.
nom.	λόγος	λόγοι
gen.	λόγου	λόγων
dat.	λόγῳ	λόγοις
acc.	λόγον	λόγους
vocative	λόγε*	

* Vocative case was used in direct address. Greek normally used the nominative for this

ὁδός, -οῦ, ἡ, *way, road* (fem.)

	sg.	pl.
nom.	ὁδός	ὁδοί
gen.	ὁδοῦ	ὁδῶν
dat.	ὁδῷ	ὁδοῖς
acc.	ὁδόν	ὁδούς
vocative	ὁδέ	

2. Neuter *nouns differ from masculine and feminine in nom. and acc. only*

δῶρον, -ου, τό, *gift*

	sg.	pl.
nom.	δῶρον	δῶρα
gen.	δώρου	δώρων
dat.	δώρῳ	δώροις
acc.	δῶρον	δῶρα

C. Substantives Using First and Second Declension Forms

1. Definite Article, the

	sg.			pl.		
	m.	f.	n.	m.	f.	n.
nom.	ὁ	ἡ	τό	οἱ	αἱ	τά
gen.	τοῦ	τῆς	τοῦ	τῶν	τῶν	τῶν
dat.	τῷ	τῇ	τῷ	τοῖς	ταῖς	τοῖς
acc.	τόν	τήν	τό	τούς	τάς	τά

---

purpose; distinct vocative forms existed only for singular second declension masculine and feminine nouns and for a few singular third declension nouns, and even for them, the nominative was sometimes used.

2. Relative Pronoun, who, whose, whom, which, that

	sg.			pl.		
	m.	f.	n.	m.	f.	n.
nom.	ὅς	ἥ	ὅ	οἵ	αἵ	ἅ
gen.	οὗ	ἧς	οὗ	ὧν	ὧν	ὧν
dat.	ᾧ	ᾗ	ᾧ	οἷς	αἷς	οἷς
acc.	ὅν	ἥν	ὅ	οὕς	ἅς	ἅ

3. Demonstrative Pronouns

ἐκεῖνος, -η, -ο, that, pl. those

	sg.			pl.		
	m.	f.	n.	m.	f.	n.
nom.	ἐκεῖνος	ἐκείνη	ἐκεῖνο	ἐκεῖνοι	ἐκεῖναι	ἐκεῖνα
gen.	ἐκείνου	ἐκείνης	ἐκείνου	ἐκείνων	ἐκείνων	ἐκείνων
dat.	ἐκείνῳ	ἐκείνῃ	ἐκείνῳ	ἐκείνοις	ἐκείναις	ἐκείνοις
acc.	ἐκεῖνον	ἐκείνην	ἐκεῖνο	ἐκείνους	ἐκείνας	ἐκεῖνα

οὗτος, αὕτη, τοῦτο, this, pl. these

	sg.			pl.		
	m.	f.	n.	m.	f.	n.
nom.	οὗτος	αὕτη	τοῦτο	οὗτοι	αὗται	ταῦτα
gen.	τούτου	ταύτης	τούτου	τούτων	τούτων	τούτων
dat.	τούτῳ	ταύτῃ	τούτῳ	τούτοις	ταύταις	τούτοις
acc.	τοῦτον	ταύτην	τοῦτο	τούτους	ταύτας	ταῦτα

4. *Adjectives of the first and second declensions. "Three-ending" adjectives distinguish all three genders; "two-ending" adjectives use only second declension forms and combine the masc. and fem. genders.*

δίκαιος, -α, -ον, *just, righteous*

	sg.			pl.		
	m.	f.	n.	m.	f.	n.
nom.	δίκαιος	δικαία	δίκαιον	δίκαιοι	δίκαιαι	δίκαια
gen.	δικαίου	δικαίας	δικαίου	δικαίων	δικαίων	δικαίων
dat.	δικαίῳ	δικαίᾳ	δικαίῳ	δικαίοις	δικαίαις	δικαίοις
acc.	δίκαιον	δικαίαν	δίκαιον	δικαίους	δικαίας	δίκαια

πιστός, -ή, -όν, *faithful*

	sg.			pl.		
	m.	f.	n.	m.	f.	n.
nom.	πιστός	πιστή	πιστόν	πιστοί	πισταί	πιστά
gen.	πιστοῦ	πιστῆς	πιστοῦ	πιστῶν	πιστῶν	πιστῶν
dat.	πιστῷ	πιστῇ	πιστῷ	πιστοῖς	πισταῖς	πιστοῖς
acc.	πιστόν	πιστήν	πιστόν	πιστούς	πιστάς	πιστά

αἰώνιος, -ον, *eternal, agelong*

	sg.		pl.	
	m. / f.	n.	m. / f.	n.
nom.	αἰώνιος	αἰώνιον	αἰώνιοι	αἰώνια
gen.	αἰωνίου	αἰωνίου	αἰωνίων	αἰωνίων
dat.	αἰωνίῳ	αἰωνίῳ	αἰωνίοις	αἰωνίοις
acc.	αἰώνιον	αἰώνιον	αἰωνίους	αἰώνια

D. Nouns of the Third Declension

χείρ, -ός, ἡ, *hand*

	sg.	pl.
nom.	χείρ	χεῖρες
gen.	χειρός	χειρῶν
dat.	χειρί	χερσί(ν)
acc.	χεῖρα	χεῖρας

πατήρ, πατρός, ὁ, *father*

	s.	pl.
nom.	πατήρ	πατέρες
gen.	πατρός	πατέρων
dat.	πατρί	πατράσι(ν)
acc.	πατέρα	πατέρας
voc.	πάτερ	

ὄνομα, ὀνόματος, τό, *name*

	sg.	pl.
nom.	ὄνομα	ὀνόματα
gen.	ὀνόματος	ὀνομάτων
dat.	ὀνόματι	ὀνόμασι(ν)
acc.	ὄνομα	ὀνόματα

φῶς, φωτός, τό, *light*

	sg.	pl.
nom.	φῶς	φῶτα
gen.	φωτός	φωτῶν
dat.	φωτί	φωσί(ν)
acc.	φῶς	φῶτα

κρίσις, κρίσεως, ἡ, *judgment*

	sg.	pl.
nom.	κρίσις	κρίσεις
gen.	κρίσεως	κρίσεων
dat.	κρίσει	κρίσεσι(ν)
acc.	κρίσιν	κρίσεις
voc.	κρίσι	

σκότος,* σκότους, τό, *darkness*

	sg.	pl.
nom.	σκότος	σκότη [σκότε-α]
gen.	σκότους [σκότε-ος]	σκοτῶν [σκοτέ-ων]
dat.	σκότει	σκότεσι
acc.	σκότος	σκότη [σκότε-α]

E. Other Substantives Using Third Declension Forms

1. Interrogative and indefinite pronouns

τίς, τί, *what? who?*

	sg.		pl.	
	m. / f.	n.	m. / f.	n.
nom.	τίς	τί	τίνες	τίνα
gen.	τίνος		τίνων	
dat.	τίνι		τίσι	
acc.	τίνα	τί	τίνας	τίνα

τις, τι, *someone, something*

	sg.		pl.	
	m. / f.	n.	m. / f.	n
nom.	τις	τι	τινές	τινά
gen.	τινός		τινῶν	
dat.	τινί		τισί(ν)	
acc.	τινά	τι	τινάς	τινά

---

* Nouns of this type (which are fairly numerous) have apparently undergone contraction. Presumed uncontracted forms are given in brackets to show the normal third declension endings.

2. Substantives combining first and third declension forms

πᾶς, πᾶσα, πᾶν, all, every

	sg.			pl.		
	m.	f.	n.	m.	f.	n.
nom.	πᾶς	πᾶσα	πᾶν	πάντες	πᾶσαι	πάντα
gen.	παντός	πάσης	παντός	πάντων	πασῶν	πάντων
dat.	παντί	πάσῃ	παντί	πᾶσι(ν)	πάσαις	πᾶσι(ν)
acc.	πάντα	πᾶσαν	πᾶν	πάντας	πάσας	πάντα

εἷς, μία, ἕν, one

	m.	f.	n.
nom.	εἷς	μία	ἕν
gen.	ἑνός	μιᾶς	ἑνός
dat.	ἑνί	μιᾷ	ἑνί
acc.	ἕνα	μίαν	ἕν

F. Personal Pronouns

First person:

	sg.	pl.
nom.	ἐγώ	ἡμεῖς
gen.	ἐμοῦ, μου	ἡμῶν
dat.	ἐμοί, μοι	ἡμῖν
acc.	ἐμέ, με	ἡμᾶς

Second person:

	sg.	pl.
nom.	σύ	ὑμεῖς
gen.	σοῦ	ὑμῶν
dat.	σοί	ὑμῖν
acc.	σέ	ὑμᾶς

Third person (also the intensive pronoun):

	sg.			pl.		
	m.	f.	n.	m.	f.	n.
nom.	αὐτός	αὐτή	αὐτό	αὐτοί	αὐταί	αὐτά
gen.	αὐτοῦ	αὐτῆς	αὐτοῦ	αὐτῶν	αὐτῶν	αὐτῶν
dat.	αὐτῷ	αὐτῇ	αὐτῷ	αὐτοῖς	αὐταῖς	αὐτοῖς
acc.	αὐτόν	αὐτήν	αὐτό	αὐτούς	αὐτάς	αὐτά

G. Comparison of Adjectives

Simple	Comparative	Superlative
A πιστός, -ή, -όν faithful	πιστότερος, -α, -ον	πιστότατος, -η, -ον
B κακός, -ή, -όν bad	κακίων, -ον (gen. κακίονος)	κάκιστος, -η, -ον

II. Verbs

A. εἰμί, *be*

Present Tense

	Indicative		Subjunctive		Imperative	
	sg.	pl.	sg.	pl.	sg.	pl.
1	εἰμί	ἐσμέν	ὦ	ὦμεν		
2	εἶ	ἐστέ	ᾖς	ἦτε	ἴσθι	ἔστε
3	ἐστί(ν)	εἰσί(ν)	ᾖ	ὦσι(ν)	ἔστω, ἤτω	ἔστωσαν, ἔστων

Infinitive: εἶναι

Present Participle

	sg.			pl.		
	m.	f.	n.	m.	f.	n.
nom.	ὤν	οὖσα	ὄν	ὄντες	οὖσαι	ὄντα
gen.	ὄντος	οὔσης	ὄντος	ὄντων	οὐσῶν	ὄντων
dat.	ὄντι	οὔσῃ	ὄντι	οὖσι(ν)	οὔσαις	οὖσι(ν)
acc.	ὄντα	οὖσαν	ὄν	ὄντας	οὔσας	ὄντα

Imperfect Indicative		**Future Indicative**	
sg.	pl.	sg.	pl.
1 ἤμην, ἦν	ἦμεν	ἔσομαι	ἐσόμεθα
2 ἦς, ἦσθα	ἦτε	ἔσῃ	ἔσεσθε
3 ἦν	ἦσαν	ἔσται	ἔσονται

B. Tenses of the O-Verb
(For participles see section C.)

Present Active

Indicative		**Subjunctive**		**Imperative**	
sg.	pl.	sg.	pl.	sg.	pl.
1 λύω	λύομεν	λύω	λύωμεν		
2 λύεις	λύετε	λύῃς	λύητε	λῦε	λύετε
3 λύει	λύουσι(ν)	λύῃ	λύωσι(ν)	λυέτω	λυόντων, λυέτωσαν

Infinitive: λύειν

Imperfect Active Indicative		**Future Active Indicative**	
sg.	pl.	sg.	pl.
1 ἔλυον	ἐλύομεν	λύσω	λύσομεν
2 ἔλυες	ἐλύετε	λύσεις	λύσετε
3 ἔλυε	ἔλυον	λύσει	λύσουσι(ν)

Future Infinitive: λύσειν

Aorist Active

Indicative		**Subjunctive**		**Imperative**	
1 ἔλυσα	ἐλύσαμεν	λύσω	λύσωμεν		
2 ἔλυσας	ἐλύσατε	λύσῃς	λύσητε	λῦσον	λύσατε
3 ἔλυσε	ἔλυσαν	λύσῃ	λύσωσι(ν)	λυσάτω	λυσάντων, λυσάτωσαν

Infinitive: λῦσαι

	Perfect Active Indicative		Pluperfect Active Indicative*	
	sg.	pl.	sg.	pl.
1	λέλυκα	λελύκαμεν	ἐλελύκειν	ἐλελύκειμεν
2	λέλυκας	λελύκατε	ἐλελύκεις	ἐλελύκειτε
3	λέλυκε	λελύκασι(ν)	ἐλελύκει	ἐλελύκεισαν

Perfect Active Infinitive: λελυκέναι

Present Middle-Passive

	Indicative		Subjunctive		Imperative	
	sg.	pl.	sg.	pl.	sg.	pl.
1	λύομαι	λυόμεθα	λύωμαι	λυώμεθα		
2	λύῃ	λύεσθε	λύῃ	λύησθε	λύου	λύεσθε
3	λύεται	λύονται	λύηται	λύωνται	λυέσθω	λυέσθων, λυέσθωσαν

Infinitive: λύεσθαι

Imperfect Middle-Passive Indicative

1	ἐλυόμην	ἐλυόμεθα
2	ἐλύου	ἐλύεσθε
3	ἐλύετο	ἐλύοντο

	Future Middle Indicative		Future Passive Indicative	
	sg.	pl.	sg.	pl.
1	λύσομαι	λυσόμεθα	λυθήσομαι	λυθησόμεθα
2	λύσῃ	λύσεσθε	λυθήσῃ	λυθήσεσθε
3	λύσεται	λύσονται	λυθήσεται	λυθήσονται

Future Middle
Infinitive: λύσεσθαι

Future Passive
Infinitive: λυθήσεσθαι

Aorist Middle

	Indicative		Subjunctive		Imperative	
1	ἐλυσάμην	ἐλυσάμεθα	λύσωμαι	λυσώμεθα		
2	ἐλύσω	ἐλύσασθε	λύσῃ	λύσησθε	λῦσαι	λύσασθε
3	ἐλύσατο	ἐλύσαντο	λύσηται	λύσωνται	λυσάσθω	λυσάσθων, λυσάσθωσαν

Infinitive: λύσασθαι

* Sometimes the augment was dropped.

Aorist Passive

	Indicative		Subjunctive		Imperative	
	sg.	pl.	sg.	pl.	sg.	pl.
1	ἐλύθην	ἐλύθημεν	λυθῶ	λυθῶμεν		
2	ἐλύθης	ἐλύθητε	λυθῇς	λυθῆτε	λύθητι	λύθητε
3	ἐλύθη	ἐλύθησαν	λυθῇ	λυθῶσι(ν)	λυθήτω	λυθέντων, λυθήτωσαν

Infinitive: λυθῆναι

Perfect Middle-Passive

Indicative

	sg.	pl.
1	λέλυμαι	λελύμεθα
2	λέλυσαι	λέλυσθε
3	λέλυται	λέλυνται

Infinitive: λελύσθαι

Pluperfect Middle-Passive

This tense did exist in the indicative, but was more likely to be constructed "periphrastically" by combining the perfect middle-passive participle with the imperfect of εἰμί, e.g., λελυμένος ἤμην.

C. Participles of the O-Verb

Present Active

	sg.			pl.		
	m.	f.	n.	m.	f.	n.
nom.	λύων	λύουσα	λῦον	λύοντες	λύουσαι	λύοντα
gen.	λύοντος	λυούσης	λύοντος	λυόντων	λυουσῶν	λυόντων
dat.	λύοντι	λυούσῃ	λύοντι	λύουσι(ν)	λυούσαις	λύουσι(ν)
acc.	λύοντα	λύουσαν	λῦον	λύοντας	λυούσας	λύοντα

Present Middle-Passive

	sg.			pl.		
	m.	f.	n.	m.	f.	n.
nom.	λυόμενος	λυομένη	λυόμενον	λυόμενοι	λυόμεναι	λυόμενα
gen.	λυομένου	λυομένης	λυομένου	λυομένων	λυομένων	λυομένων
dat.	λυομένῳ	λυομένῃ	λυομένῳ	λυομένοις	λυομέναις	λυομένοις
acc.	λυόμενον	λυομένην	λυόμενον	λυομένους	λυομένας	λυόμενα

Future Active

	sg.		
	m.	f.	n.
nom.	λύσων	λύσουσα	λῦσον
gen.	λύσοντος	λυσούσης	λύσοντος

κ.τ.λ. (like present active with addition of -σ- infix)

Future Middle

	sg.		
	m.	f.	n.
nom.	λυσόμενος	λυσομένη	λυσόμενον
gen.	λυσομένου	λυσομένης	λυσομένου

κ.τ.λ. (like present middle-passive with addition of -σ- infix)

Future Passive

	sg.		
	m.	f.	n.
nom.	λυθησόμενος	λυθησομένη	λυθησόμενον
gen.	λυθησομένου	λυθησομένης	λυθησομένου

κ.τ.λ. (like present middle-passive with addition of -θησ- infix)

Aorist Active

	sg.			pl.		
	m.	f.	n.	m.	f.	n.
nom.	λύσας	λύσασα	λῦσαν	λύσαντες	λύσασαι	λύσαντα
gen.	λύσαντος	λυσάσης	λύσαντος	λυσάντων	λυσασῶν	λυσάντων
dat.	λύσαντι	λυσάσῃ	λύσαντι	λύσασι(ν)	λυσάσαις	λύσασι(ν)
acc.	λύσαντα	λύσασαν	λῦσαν	λύσαντας	λυσάσας	λύσαντα

Aorist Middle

	sg.		
	m.	f.	n.
nom.	λυσάμενος	λυσαμένη	λυσάμενον
gen.	λυσαμένου	λυσαμένης	λυσαμένου

κ.τ.λ. (like present middle-passive except with -σ- infix and -α- theme vowel)

Aorist Passive

	sg.			pl.		
	m.	f.	n.	m.	f.	n.
nom.	λυθείς	λυθεῖσα	λυθέν	λυθέντες	λυθεῖσαι	λυθέντα
gen.	λυθέντος	λυθείσης	λυθέντος	λυθέντων	λυθεισῶν	λυθέντων
dat.	λυθέντι	λυθείσῃ	λυθέντι	λυθεῖσι(ν)	λυθείσαις	λυθεῖσι(ν)
acc.	λυθέντα	λυθεῖσαν	λυθέν	λυθέντας	λυθείσας	λυθέντα

Second Aorist Active (of εἶδον; like present active except for accentuation)

	sg.			pl.		
	m.	f.	n.	m.	f.	n.
nom.	ἰδών	ἰδοῦσα	ἰδόν	ἰδόντες	ἰδοῦσαι	ἰδόντα
gen.	ἰδόντος	ἰδούσης	ἰδόντος	ἰδόντων	ἰδουσῶν	ἰδόντων
dat.	ἰδόντι	ἰδούσῃ	ἰδόντι	ἰδοῦσι(ν)	ἰδούσαις	ἰδοῦσι(ν)
acc.	ἰδόντα	ἰδοῦσαν	ἰδόν	ἰδόντας	ἰδούσας	ἰδόντα

Perfect Active

	sg.			pl.		
	m.	f.	n.	m.	f.	n.
nom.	λελυκώς	λελυκυῖα	λελυκός	λελυκότες	λελυκυῖαι	λελυκότα
gen.	λελυκότος	λελυκυίας	λελυκότος	λελυκότων	λελυκυιῶν	λελυκότων
dat.	λελυκότι	λελυκυίᾳ	λελυκότι	λελυκόσι(ν)	λελυκυίαις	λελυκόσι(ν)
acc.	λελυκότα	λελυκυῖαν	λελυκός	λελυκότας	λελυκυίας	λελυκότα

Perfect Middle-Passive

	sg.			pl.		
	m.	f.	n.	m.	f.	n.
nom.	λελυμένος	λελυμένη	λελυμένον	λελυμένοι	λελυμέναι	λελυμένα
gen.	λελυμένου	λελυμένης	λελυμένου	λελυμένων	λελυμένων	λελυμένων
dat.	λελυμένῳ	λελυμένῃ	λελυμένῳ	λελυμένοις	λελυμέναις	λελυμένοις
acc.	λελυμένον	λελυμένην	λελυμένον	λελυμένους	λελυμένας	λελυμένα

D. Contract Verbs

Results of basic vowel contractions

α + ε = α	ε + ε = ει	ο + ε = ου
α + ει = ᾳ*	ε + ει = ει	ο + ει = οι
α + η = α	ε + η = η	ο + η = ω
α + η = ᾳ	ε + η = η	ο + η = οι
α + ο = ω	ε + ο = ου	ο + ο = ου
α + ου = ω	ε + ου = ου	ο + ου = ου
α + ω = ω	ε + ω = ω	ο + ω = ω

The presumed uncontracted forms will be given in parentheses with the paradigm of the α-contract verb only.

A-*Contract Verb*

ἀγαπάω, *love, cherish, favor*

Present Active

Indicative and subjunctive (identical in α-contract verbs):

	sg.	pl.
1	ἀγαπῶ [ἀγαπάω]	ἀγαπῶμεν [ἀγαπάομεν, -άωμεν]
2	ἀγαπᾷς [ἀγαπάεις, -άῃς]	ἀγαπᾶτε [ἀγαπάετε, -άητε]
3	ἀγαπᾷ [ἀγαπάει, -αη]	ἀγαπῶσι [ἀγαπάουσι, -άωσι]

Infinitive: ἀγαπᾶν [ἀγαπάειν, from ἀγαπαεεν]

Imperfect Active Indicative

	sg.	pl.
1	ἠγάπων [ἠγάπαον]	ἠγαπῶμεν [ἠγαπάομεν]
2	ἠγάπας [ἠγάπαες]	ἠγαπᾶτε [ἠγαπάετε]
3	ἠγάπα [ἠγάπαε]	ἠγάπων [ἠγάπαον]

* α (without ι-subscript) in present active infinitive.

Present Middle-Passive

Indicative and subjunctive (identical in α-contract verbs)

sg.	pl.
1 ἀγαπῶμαι [ἀγαπάομαι, -άωμαι]	ἀγαπώμεθα [ἀγαπαόμεθα, -αώμεθα]
2 ἀγαπᾷ [ἀγαπάῃ]	ἀγαπᾶσθε [ἀγαπάεσθε, -άησθε]
3 ἀγαπᾶται [ἀγαπάεται, -άηται]	ἀγαπῶνται [ἀγαπάονται, -άωνται]

Infinitive: ἀγαπᾶσθαι [ἀγαπάεσθαι]

Imperfect Middle-Passive Indicative

1 ἠγαπώμην [ἠγαπαόμην]	ἠγαπώμεθα [ἠγαπαόμεθα]
2 ἠγαπῶ [ἠγαπάου]	ἠγαπᾶσθε [ἠγαπάεσθε]
3 ἠγαπᾶτο [ἠγαπάετο]	ἠγαπῶντο [ἠγαπάοντο]

Other Principal Parts

Fut. Act.: ἀγαπήσω
Aor. Act.: ἠγάπησα
Perf. Act.: ἠγάπηκα
Aor. Pass.: ἠγαπήθην

E-*Contract Verb*

Present Active

Indicative		Subjunctive	
sg.	pl.	sg.	pl.
1 ποιῶ	ποιοῦμεν	ποιῶ	ποιῶμεν
2 ποιεῖς	ποιεῖτε	ποιῇς	ποιῆτε
3 ποιεῖ	ποιοῦσι	ποιῇ	ποιῶσι

Infinitive: ποιεῖν

Imperfect Active Indicative

1 ἐποίουν	ἐποιοῦμεν
2 ἐποίεις	ἐποιεῖτε
3 ἐποίει	ἐποίουν

Present Middle-Passive

Indicative		Subjunctive	
sg.	pl.	sg.	pl.
1 ποιοῦμαι	ποιούμεθα	ποιῶμαι	ποιώμεθα
2 ποιῇ	ποιεῖσθε	ποιῇ	ποιῆσθε
3 ποιεῖται	ποιοῦνται	ποιῆται	ποιῶνται

Infinitive: ποιεῖσθαι

Imperfect Middle-Passive Indicative

sg.	pl.
1 ἐποιούμην	ἐποιούμεθα
2 ἐποιοῦ	ἐποιεῖσθε
3 ἐποιεῖτο	ἐποιοῦντο

Other Principal Parts

Fut. Act.: ποιήσω
Aor. Act.: ἐποίησα
Perf. Act.: πεποίηκα
Aor. Pass.: ἐποιήθην

O-Contract Verb

Present Active

Indicative		Subjunctive	
sg.	pl.	sg.	pl.
1 δηλῶ	δηλοῦμεν	δηλῶ	δηλῶμεν
2 δηλοῖς	δηλοῦτε	δηλοῖς	δηλῶτε
3 δηλοῖ	δηλοῦσι	δηλοῖ	δηλῶσι

Infinitive: δηλοῦν

Imperfect Active Indicative

sg.	pl.
1 ἐδήλουν	ἐδηλοῦμεν
2 ἐδήλους	ἐδηλοῦτε
3 ἐδήλου	ἐδήλουν

Present Middle-Passive

Indicative		Subjunctive	
sg.	pl.	sg.	pl.
1 δηλοῦμαι	δηλούμεθα	δηλῶμαι	δηλώμεθα
2 δηλοῖ	δηλοῦσθε	δηλοῖ	δηλῶσθε
3 δηλοῦται	δηλοῦνται	δηλῶται	δηλῶνται

Infinitive: δηλοῦσθαι

Imperfect Middle-Passive Indicative

	sg.	pl.
1	ἐδηλούμην	ἐδηλούμεθα
2	ἐδηλοῦ	ἐδηλοῦσθε
3	ἐδηλοῦτο	ἐδηλοῦντο

Other Principal Parts

Fut. Act.:   δηλώσω
Aor. Act.:   ἐδήλωσα
Perf. Act.:   δεδήλωκα
Aor. Pass.:   ἐδηλώθην

E. MI-Verbs: Two Examples

Present Active Indicative

	sg.	pl.	sg.	pl.
1	δίδωμι	δίδομεν	ἵστημι	ἵσταμεν
2	δίδως	δίδοτε	ἵστης	ἵστατε
3	δίδωσι	διδόασι(ν)	ἵστησι	ἱστᾶσι(ν)

Present Active Subjunctive

	sg.	pl.	sg.	pl.
1	διδῶ	διδῶμεν	ἱστῶ	ἱστῶμεν
2	διδῷς	διδῶτε	ἱστῇς	ἱστῆτε
3	διδῷ	διδῶσι	ἱστῇ	ἱστῶσι

Imperfect Active Indicative

	sg.	pl.		sg.	pl.
1	ἐδίδουν	ἐδίδομεν		ἵστην	ἵσταμεν
2	ἐδίδους	ἐδίδοτε		ἵστης	ἵστατε
3	ἐδίδου	ἐδίδοσαν		ἵστη	ἵστασαν

Present Middle-Passive Indicative

	sg.	pl.		sg.	pl.
1	δίδομαι	διδόμεθα		ἵσταμαι	ἱστάμεθα
2	δίδοσαι	δίδοσθε		ἵστασαι	ἵστασθε
3	δίδοται	δίδονται		ἵσταται	ἵστανται

Present Middle-Passive Subjunctive

	sg.	pl.		sg.	pl.
1	διδῶμαι	διδώμεθα		ἱστῶμαι	ἱστώμεθα
2	διδῷ	διδῶσθε		ἱστῇ	ἱστῆσθε
3	διδῶται	διδῶνται		ἱστῆται	ἱστῶνται

Imperfect Middle-Passive Indicative

	sg.	pl.		sg.	pl.
1	ἐδιδόμην	ἐδιδόμεθα		ἱστάμην	ἱστάμεθα
2	ἐδίδοσο	ἐδίδοσθε		ἵστασο	ἵστασθε
3	ἐδίδοτο	ἐδίδοντο		ἵστατο	ἵσταντο

Other Tenses

Fut. Act.	δώσω	στήσω
Aor. Act.	ἔδωκα	ἔστησα, ἔστην
Aor. Mid.	ἐδόμην	ἐστησάμην
Perf. Act.	δέδωκα	ἕστηκα
Aor. Pass.	ἐδόθην	ἐστάθην

III. Principal Parts of Irregular Verbs

Pres. Act.	Fut. Act.	Aor. Act.	Perf. Act.	Perf. Pass.	Aor. Pass.	
ἀγγέλλω	ἀγγελῶ	ἤγγειλα	ἤγγελκα	ἤγγελμαι	ἠγγέλθην	report
ἄγω	ἄξω	ἤγαγον	ἦχα	ἦγμαι	ἤχθην	lead
αἱρέω	αἱρήσω	εἷλον	ᾕρηκα	ᾕρημαι	ᾑρέθην	take
αἴρω	ἀρῶ	ἦρα	ἦρκα	ἦρμαι	ἤρθην	lift
ἀκούω	ἀκούσω, ἀκούσομαι	ἤκουσα	ἀκήκοα	ἤκουσμαι	ἠκούσθην	hear
ἁμαρτάνω	ἁμαρτήσω	ἥμαρτον	ἡμάρτηκα		ἡμαρτήθην	sin
ἀνοίγω	ἀνοίξω	ἤνοιξα, ἀνέῳξα		ἀνέῳγμαι	ἀνεῴχθην, ἠνοίχθην	open
ἀπόλλυμι	ἀπολέσω, ἀπολῶ	ἀπώλεσα	ἀπολώλεκα			destroy
ἀποστέλλω	ἀποστελῶ	ἀπέστειλα	ἀπέσταλκα	ἀπέσταλμαι	ἀπεστάλην	send
βαίνω	βήσομαι	ἔβην	βέβηκα			go
βάλλω	βαλῶ	ἔβαλον	βέβληκα	βέβλημαι	ἐβλήθην	throw
βούλομαι	βουλήσομαι			ἐβουλήθην		will
γίνομαι	γενήσομαι	ἐγενόμην	γέγονα	γεγένημαι	ἐγενήθην	become
γινώσκω	γνώσομαι	ἔγνων	ἔγνωκα	ἔγνωσμαι	ἐγνώσθην	know
γράφω	γράψω	ἔγραψα	γέγραφα	γέγραμμαι	ἐγράφην	write
διδάσκω	διδάξω	ἐδίδαξα	δεδίδαχα	δεδίδαγμαι	ἐδιδάχθην	teach

διώκω	διώξω	ἐδίωξα	δεδίωχα	δεδίωγμαι	ἐδιώχθην	pursue
δύναμαι	δυνήσομαι				ἠδυνήθην	can, be able
ἐγείρω	ἐγερῶ	ἤγειρα	ἐγήγορα	ἐγήγερμαι	ἠγέρθην	raise
ἔρχομαι	ἐλεύσομαι	ἦλθον	ἐλήλυθα			come
ἐσθίω	φάγομαι, ἔδομαι	ἔφαγον				eat
εὑρίσκω	εὑρήσω	εὗρον	εὕρηκα	εὕρημαι	εὑρέθην	find
ἔχω	ἕξω	ἔσχον	ἔσχηκα	ἔσχημαι		have
θνῄσκω	θανοῦμαι	ἔθανον	τέθνηκα			die
καλέω	καλέσω	ἐκάλεσα	κέκληκα	κέκλημαι	ἐκλήθην	call
κρίνω	κρινῶ	ἔκρινα	κέκρικα	κέκριμαι	ἐκρίθην	judge
λαμβάνω	λήμψομαι	ἔλαβον	εἴληφα	εἴλημμαι	ἐλήμφθην	take
λέγω	ἐρῶ	εἶπον, εἶπα	εἴρηκα	εἴρημαι	ἐρρέθην	say
μένω	μενῶ	ἔμεινα	μεμένηκα			remain
ὁράω	ὄψομαι	εἶδον	ἑόρακα		ὤφθην	see
πάσχω	πείσομαι	ἔπαθον	πέπονθα			suffer
πίπτω	πεσοῦμαι	ἔπεσον	πέπτωκα			fall
στρέφω	στρέψω	ἔστρεψα		ἔστραμμαι	ἐστράφην	turn
σῴζω	σώσω	ἔσωσα	σέσωκα	σέσωσμαι	ἐσώθην	save
τάσσω	τάξω	ἔταξα	τέταχα	τέταγμαι	ἐτάχθην	arrange
φέρω	οἴσω	ἤνεγκα	ἐνήνοχα	ἐνήνεγμαι	ἠνέχθην	carry

IV. Accentuation: A Simplified Account

A. Syllables and Individual Accents

Accents can appear only on the final three syllables of a word. The formal grammatical names of these three syllables are, in order: *antepenult* ("before the penult"), *penult* ("almost last"), and *ultima* ("last").

Every syllable in Greek is either long or short, and this quality affects the distribution of accents. For purposes of accent, a syllable is long when it contains a long vowel (η or ω, sometimes α, ι, or υ) or a diphthong (except that αι or οι at the end of a word are short).

There are three accent marks and each type of accent makes its own particular demands:

˜ The circumflex accent will appear only on long syllables, only on the penult or ultima, and on the penult only if the ultima is short:

δῶρον   long penult followed by short ultima
φῶς   long ultima

´ The acute accent can appear on any of the three final syllables, provided the ultima is short; if the ultima is long, it can appear on either of the final two:*

λύοντος   short ultima
νεανίαι   short ultima
ὁδός   short ultima
λυόντων   long ultima
αὐτούς   long ultima

` The grave accent appears only on the ultima and replaces an acute accent on the ultima whenever another word follows immediately. Some small words, called "enclitics," cause an exception to this rule by giving up their accent to the preceding word. E.g., ἡ ὁδός μου, *my road*.

---

* An apparent exception is sg. and pl. genitives of nouns like κρίσις (see above, p. 182), κρίσεως, κρίσεων. Probably the ε was not felt as a full syllable.

B. Accents on Substantives

Accents on substantives tend to remain on the same syllable throughout the paradigm unless they are forced to move or change by changes in the final syllable(s). For example:

οὗτος, αὕτη, τοῦτο

Here, the accent can remain on the same syllable throughout. But when the accent falls on a long penult, it is circumflex when the ultima is short (e.g., οὗτος) and acute when the ultima is long (e.g., αὕτη).

ἄνθρωπος, ἀνθρώπου

Here, the accent falls on the antepenult where possible, that is, in forms where the ultima is short (e.g., ἄνθρωπος). It must shift to the penult when the ultima is long (e.g., ἀνθρώπου).

ὄνομα, ὀνόματος

Here, the ending adds a syllable and the accent moves to reflect this change, since it can fall no further back than the antepenult.

There are two exceptions to this general rule for accents on substantives: (1) In the first declension, the genitive plural is always -ῶν, no matter where the accent would otherwise fall. For example, δοξῶν is the genitive plural of δόξα. This exception is more apparent than real, however, since -ῶν is really a contraction of an archaic -άων. (2) Genitive and dative cases tend to behave somewhat independently of nominative and accusative. In the first and second declensions, if a substantive is accented on the ultima, it will have acute accents in the nominative and accusative, even on long syllables, but circumflex accents in the genitive and dative (see the paradigms of ἀρχή and ὁδός on pp. 177 and 179 above). In the third declension, some nouns shift their accent to the case ending in the genitive and dative (e.g., φῶς, φωτός, φωτί; πατήρ, πατρός, πατρί).

C. Accents on Verbs

Verb forms usually have what is called "recessive accent." That is to say, their accents will move as far from the ultima as they can. There are some exceptions with regard to participles (which are, after all, basically substantives), but the principle holds good elsewhere. For example:

λύω

This is the shortest possible verb form, with a long ultima.

λῦε

Since the υ of the stem happens to be long, the short ultima (ε) allows a circumflex to be used.

ἔλυον, λέλυκα

An augment or reduplication allows the accent to move further back.

λύομαι

Here a two-syllable ending and a short ultima allow the accent to stay put.

ἐλυόμην

Here a long ultima forces the accent to move.

λυόμεθα

Here a three-syllable ending forces the accent to move.

ABBREVIATIONS

κ.τ.λ.	καὶ τὰ λοιπά, and the rest, *et cetera*
acc.	accusative
act.	active
adj.	adjective
adv.	adverb
aor.	aorist
B.C.E.	Before the Common Era (current scholarly usage for B.C.)
C.E.	Common Era (current scholarly usage for A.D.)
dat.	dative
d.o.	direct object
f., fem.	feminine
fut.	future
gen.	genitive
impf.	imperfect
impv.	imperative
indic.	indicative
inf.	infinitive
i.o.	indirect object
irreg.	irregular
m., masc.	masculine
mid.	middle (voice)
ms. / mss.	manuscript / manuscripts
n., neut.	neuter
nom.	nominative
obj.	object
pass.	passive

perf.	perfect
pl.	plural
pluperf.	pluperfect
pl.	plural
pred.	predicate
prep.	preposition
pres.	present
RSV	Revised Standard Version
sg.	singular
subj.	subjunctive
s.v.	*sub verbo,* under the word/entry

GLOSSARY AND INDEX

absolute a construction detached grammatically from the main clause of its sentence but modifying the main clause — see p. 159

adjective a word used to modify a noun or pronoun (adjectives can be used substantively as nouns) — see pp. 38-39, 69-70, 159

adverb a word telling how, when, where, or in what manner an action is performed — see p. 113

anarthrous lacking the definite article

antecedent the substantive (sometimes only implied) that a pronoun or demonstrative stands in place of — see p. 23

apposition a means of identifying two substantives as referring to the same thing by placing them side by side, e.g., "my *brother Fred*"

articular infinitive an infinite used with a definite article to form a subordinate clause — see pp. 166-70

attributive an adjective modifying a noun directly (cf. "predicate adjective") — see pp. 38-39

case the use of different forms of a given substantive to show its relations with other words and its roles in basic sentence structure; Greek has nominative, genitive, dative, accusative, and vocative cases — see pp. 9-12, 15-17, 38-40

clause a complete statement including subject, verb, and any other elements necessary to express the meaning; at a minimum, subject and verb are sufficient, e.g., "I am reading." Main clauses are those that can stand on their own as complete sentences; subordinate clauses are attached to a main clause by a subordinating conjunction or relative pronoun. E.g., "I am reading [main clause], while you write [subordinate clause]" — see pp. 149-52

comparison   the use of different forms of adjectives and adverbs to allow comparison of two (comparative state) or more (superlative state) things or actions, e.g., "large / largely" (simple state), "larger / more largely" (comparative state), "largest / most largely" (superlative state) — see pp. 100-102

conjugation   the display of the forms of a verb — see pp. 185-95

conjunction   a word that joins other words or clauses, either a "coordinating conjunction" (e.g., *and, but, or*) or a "subordinating conjunction" (e.g., *while, since, as, if, although*) — see pp. 149-52

declension   the use of various forms of a given substantive to indicate gender, number, and case — see pp. 24-26, 44-46

definite article   a word modifying a substantive and defining it as particular or unique; English "the" — see pp. 18-19, 179

demonstrative   a word pointing out the particular thing referred to; in English "this," "these," "that," and "those" are demonstratives — see pp. 76-77

deponent   a type of Greek verb that uses forms that normally indicate passive or middle voice as the active voice forms — see p. 86

direct object   a substantive that receives the action of a verb, e.g., "I hand you the *book*" — see pp. 10-12

enclitic   a Greek word that gives up its accent to the word preceding it — see p. 198

imperative — see mood

indicative — see mood

indirect object   a substantive indicating who "benefited" from the action of a verb, e.g., "I hand *you* the book" — see pp. 10-12

infinitive   a verbal noun, in English formed with "to," e.g., "to read" — see pp. 114-16

mood   a property of verbs that distinguishes whether a given verb is making a definite statement (indicative), indicating less certainty (subjunctive), giving a command (imperative), or embodying the verbal idea in the form of a noun (infinitive) or adjective (participle) — see pp. 70-72, 77-81, 114-16

noun   the name of a person, place, or thing — see p. 24

number   the distinction in both substantives and verbs between singular and plural (earlier Greek had separate dual forms as well) — see p. 9

paradigm   a chart of the forms of a verb or substantive — see pp. 177-95

participle — see mood

person a quality of verbs that indicates that the subject is the speaker (first person), the person spoken to (second person), or another person or thing spoken about (third person) — see pp. 9, 50-51

phrase any group of words making a coherent statement but not necessarily including a verb, e.g., "on the boat," "a funny clown"

predicate adjective an adjective describing the subject through a linking verb, e.g., "Sarah is *intelligent*" — see pp. 9-10, 38-39

predicate nominative a noun or pronoun identified with the subject through a linking verb, e.g., "Sarah is *president*" — see pp. 9-10

preposition a word governing a substantive and attaching it to a clause, e.g., "All that happened *before* the war" — see pp. 31-32

pronoun a substantive that takes the place of a noun, e.g., "she," "they," "we," "whose" — see pp. 32-34, 36-37, 44

relative pronoun a pronoun serving to link a subordinate clause to a substantive (implied or expressed), e.g., "The person *who* wrote this text . . ." — see pp. 22-24

subject the substantive whose activity or state of being is spoken of in the verb, e.g., "The *girl* is reading" — see pp. 9-12

subjunctive — see mood

substantive any noun or noun-like word, including adjectives, pronouns, and demonstratives

tense a quality of verbs that indicates the time (e.g., past, present, future) and other aspects (e.g., continuity, punctiliar quality, completeness) of an action or state of being — see pp. 55-56, 127-30, 141-43

verb a word indicating state of being (e.g., "is") or action (e.g., "read," "do," "make") — see pp. 9-12, 134-37

voice a quality of verbs that indicates whether the subject is acting or being acted on; Greek has three voices: active (subject acting), passive (subject being acted on), and middle (subject acting on itself) — see pp. 87-89

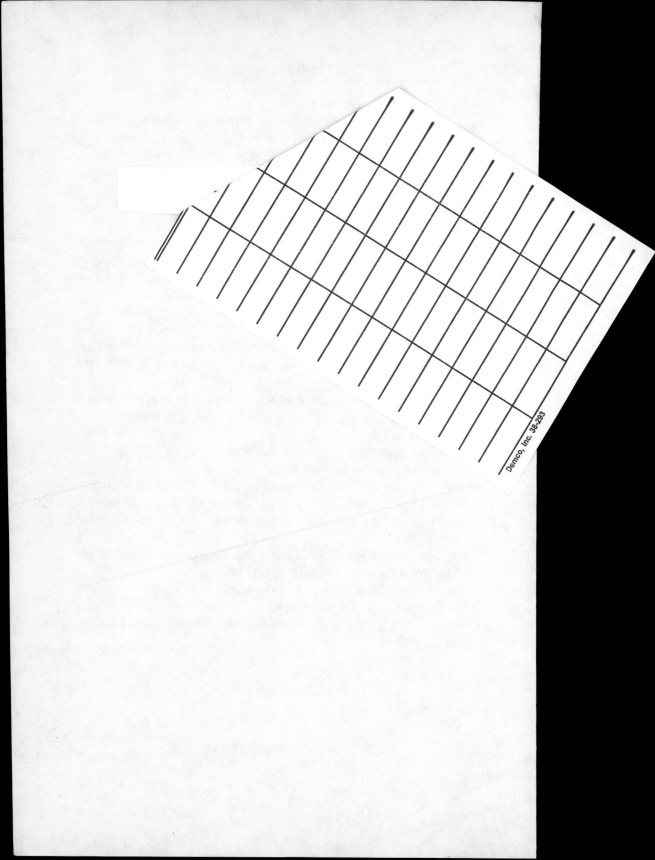